A Place of No Importance

A Place of No Importance

Veena Muthuraman

JUGGERNAUT BOOKS
KS House, 118 Shahpur Jat, New Delhi 110049, India

First published by Juggernaut Books 2016

10 9 8 7 6 5 4 3 2 1

ISBN 9788193284117

Typeset in Adobe Caslon Pro by R. Ajith Kumar, New Delhi

Printed at Replika Press Pvt. Ltd.

To my parents – for opening up worlds,
old and new

Contents

Author's Note ix

A Festive Suicide, Attempted 1
Possessed 11
God's Own Country 28
A House on Upper Street 51
A New Release 65
Scenes from a Scandal 81
A New Beginning 97
The Amman of Saris 112
A Yank in Ayyanarpatti 131
The Demon Wind of Aadi 151
Prelude to a Wedding 166
A Love Story, Starring Councillor Muthu 182
Macondo Thatha 200

Acknowledgements 207
A Note on the Author 209

Author's Note

On a late November day in 2006, my mother and I made an unplanned visit to the village where she grew up. Unlike memories of my previous trips to my parents' villages which tend to blend into one another, I vividly remember this particular visit. We disembarked at the bus stop and walked the last mile on a paved road cut between once dense forests, now lined with eucalyptus trees. There was a nip in the air as it had rained the night before. At the village, we spent the day sitting in the courtyard, and picking chillies and brinjal from the yard to take back with us. I met the requisite number of people as always but this time, I seemed to have caught them unawares as they were not expecting us. It was the first time in the almost three decades I had known this place that I realized that it changed with the seasons, and it was not always dry and parched like in the summer, and that life here goes on even when I am not around. It was also the first time I considered chronicling life in the villages that are my roots.

Years later, when I started writing the stories in this collection, it seemed only logical and natural that I write one for each month in the Tamil calendar. For centuries, life here has revolved around the seasons, the rains, the harvests and the festivals. Now it is mostly the festivals that are left as the rains fail continually and not much is sown and grown. I wanted to catch this way of life before it completely vanished, before all we have left are festivals which become meaningless and mindless because we forget why they were celebrated in the first place.

The Tamil year, similar to the Gregorian calendar, consists of twelve months and the number of days per month varies between 29 and 32. The New Year falls in Chithirai, in mid-April, but I chose to begin with the second half of the year, starting with Aipasi, the seventh month, and lead up to the main harvest in Thai before circling to the new year. I have attempted to be true to the months in that the stories, for the most part, fit within the idea of the month they are set in.

The months, in order of appearance in the book, are:

Aipasi – mid-October to mid-November

Aipasi is the month of Deepavali, the biggest festival in these parts, and hence provides a festive beginning. More important, it is the month that the torrential rains from the north-east monsoon make their entry. For the villages in this part of the Tamil country, it is these rains that determine whether the year's yield will be good or not.

Karthigai – mid-November to mid-December

Karthigai is the gentle start of winter when the days become shorter and darker; more tea is consumed and ghost stories are exchanged. It is also the month of the birth of the god Murugan, a favoured deity of the Tamils.

I should point out here that Ayyanarpatti lies in the heart of Siva country. One would be hard-pressed to find a Vishnu temple in the villages while everyone from the Saivite pantheon makes an appearance: Ganesha, Remover of Obstacles; Murugan, Protector and Lover; Durga, Kali and Kamakshi – Parvati in her many avatars; and Sivan himself. The shrines (and the villages) are usually guarded by a fierce Ayyanar, usually mounted on his horse and wielding a lance.

Markazhi – mid-December to mid-January

Temple visits are at the maximum but this month is inauspicious for weddings and celebrations. Might it be that both gods' blessings and human hands are required in the fields to reap the harvest before Thai?

Thai – mid-January to mid-February

Pongal, the Tamil harvest festival, is celebrated on the first three days of this month with offerings of first rice and cane to the gods of nature. This is the time for acquisitions – a spouse, a vehicle or, in our case, a house.

Maasi – mid-February to mid-March

The chill in the air starts to disappear as winter is on its way out. If there is sufficient water in the reservoirs, then a round of pulses and lentils is sown so that it can be harvested before peak summer.

Pankuni – mid-March to mid-April

The twelfth month in the calendar, Pankuni offers the last possibility of showers, perhaps a final opportunity to make amends, before the New Year and the onset of the unrelenting summer.

Chithirai – mid-April to mid-May

The New Year, a time for beginnings, an auspicious month but let there be no doubt – summer is here. In the Kaveri delta, a quick rice round is sometimes attempted but in rain-fed Ayyanarpatti, the summer months are lazy and languorous.

Vaikasi – mid-May to mid-June

The hottest days of the year, the dreaded Agni Natchathiram falls early this month. The wedding of god Murugan is celebrated this month with kavadi processions often culminating in a fire walk.

Aani – mid-June to mid-July

A filler month, if it can be called that. The air starts to cool down in the latter half as the south-west monsoon brings rains to the west coast.

Aadi – mid-July to mid-August

An important month as paddy seedlings are prepared and sown, and perhaps for the same reason, Aadi is an inauspicious month for weddings. A number of women-only festivals abound and women are advised to stay away from their spouses. The winds gather force and an old Tamil saying goes: the Aadi wind will move the grindstone.

Avani – mid-August to mid-September

This is an auspicious time for weddings and celebrations after the hot summer months. A smattering of showers from the receding south-west monsoon portends well for the sown paddy crop.

Purattasi – mid-September to mid-October

A month of fasting and prayers before the mayhem of Deepavali. The Sani god is believed to lose his evil powers during this month and hence ventures are likely to succeed.

~

I started writing this note to explain my choice of using the months as a device in this book but it strikes me that this may also be the right place to provide a partial explanation for why I wanted to tell these stories in the first place. The villages that Ayyanarpatti is based on is a world that is seemingly different from the narrative of emerging urban India; but my experience of it, vicarious and otherwise, tells me that despite the superficial differences, it contains within it the imprint of an aspirational nation state which is worth exploring, if only to understand the extent to which this world mirrors the one outside it. I would like to believe that the stories transport the reader to a different place where modernity and tradition seemingly collide though it will become quickly apparent that one is just co-opted into the other. A village like Ayyanarpatti is by no means an inaccessible world, just one that isn't deemed important enough to merit a place in the predominantly urban narratives we are used to. This is especially true of writing in English, and I see *A Place of No Importance* as a modest attempt in bringing about a change in this state of affairs.

Veena Muthuraman
20 February 2016
Edinburgh

A Festive Suicide, Attempted

Ayyanarpatti ran out of firecrackers by mid-afternoon on Deepavali day. The mala-wala explosives were the first to go as they were exploded synchronously just before dawn. The Shivaji and Lakshmi single 'bombs' followed, lit next to oblivious senior citizens who shuddered and covered their ears as the sound reverberated across the village. Sissy crackers – sparklers, ground chakras, flower pots – outlasted the rest but not for long. The young cracker-bursters went back to their respective homes to convince their fathers to procure more firecrackers but no one paid them any attention. The interminable celebrity interviews on the various channels were proving to be too much after the gluttonous Deepavali feast, and most of the adult citizenry was dozing in front of the television.

So when Arumugam sauntered down Upper Street with a green plastic can in one hand and a bottle of arrack in the other, he had the street all to himself. 'The world has turned lazy,' Arumugam said to himself. He held up the green can and looked at it thoughtfully. 'But they'll come out soon enough,' he muttered as he walked to Rathinam's house and poured some of the contents of the can on the kolam in the front yard. He repeated this in front of a few more houses on the street before finally reaching his house. He walked up the steps and knocked on the door. No one opened and, after a couple of minutes, he knocked louder.

'Open up. It's me!'

The TV volume went up a notch but no one came out to let him in. He gave up, and walked along the narrow passage on one side of the house and peered in through the window. The kids were sleeping, and the women – his wife and daughter – were intently staring at the screen. He headed for the bore well in the backyard, emptied what remained of the green can on the ground and filled the empty can with arrack from the bottle he was carrying. Hearing a door open, he looked up furtively. Selvi, his daughter. He quickly threw the now-empty arrack bottle to one side and held up the green can, waving it like a flag to catch her attention. Selvi saw him but took no notice. She removed a few clothes from the clothesline and went back inside, firmly closing the door behind her.

His own daughter, Arumugam seethed, wouldn't acknowledge his existence. He swiftly walked back to Upper Street. What kind of a life was his? A stray dog's life. They left food out for him every day, and a sleeping mat in the veranda, but there was nothing in the world that he could call his. His wife had not spoken to him in decades; his grandchildren ran away when they saw him; his daughter looked through him, and didn't hesitate to lift her hand to thrash him every once in a while. He thought of Selvi when she was just a little girl – her look of wonder when he took her to the textile mill where he used to work a lifetime ago now. He'd promised to weave her a pavadai for every colour that existed in this world, and she had clapped her hands in delight and hugged him tight. What had happened to his little girl? Tears stung Arumugam's bloodshot eyes. Through the haze, he noticed a girl approach. Not his little Selvi, this one looked much older.

'Hey you, Nithya, stop!'

Young Nithya braked and looked up at Arumugam in surprise. She was on her way to town to buy firecrackers, and here was this alcoholic holding up a green can like a traffic policeman holding his STOP sign. He couldn't quite stand straight, and was swaying back and forth.

'Get out of the way,' she told him. 'I don't have time to waste.'

'Watch me die before you go. I am going to drink this!'

Arumugam swung the can closer so that she could read the label. Nithya recognized it – Catch, a local pesticide.

'Mama, get out of my way.' She, like most of the villagers, was used to Arumugam's potvaliancy, and didn't really believe he was going to carry out the threat.

'You listen to me, girl. Summon everyone. I am going to drink this in front of the whole village.'

'Tiger, tiger!' Nithya laughed, referring to the story of the man who cried tiger too often only to find that no one came to his rescue when there was an actual tiger about.

'You don't believe me? Call them all. You'll see me die in front of your eyes!'

Well, what was the harm, Nithya pondered. It might enliven an otherwise listless Deepavali, and provide the perfect diversion for her stealth trip to town. She parked her bicycle and ran to the nearest house.

~

Selvi looked up from the newspaper, irritated. Someone was knocking so hard that the door was going to come unhinged.

'Open the door. This is Muthu.'

Muthu? Muthu was the local councillor, the man about the village who liked to get involved in everything that went on. Selvi had seen him an hour earlier heading to the mango grove with his band of political do-nothings, carrying loads of TASMAC alcohol. He was back in the village already? Selvi got up and walked towards the door.

'It is that man,' Rajam, her mother, said softly. 'He's up to something.'

'Thank God you're here! Arumugam annan is in a dangerous state of mind,' Muthu cried as Selvi opened the door. 'Nobody had the sense to call you until now. If I'd not been on the scene, who knows…?'

'What's wrong with him?' Selvi demanded.

'I don't know how to tell you. You have to come with me.' He pointed to a crowd up the street. 'Everyone's there.'

'What has he done, Muthu?'

'Don't ask me that, please! I pleaded with him and he's promised to do nothing until you and your mother get there. We have no time to lose.'

'Thambi, please tell us what the problem is.' It was Rajam from behind the door.

Muthu turned pale. 'How'll I tell you? It is a question

of your thali. It's swinging in the wind.' He swung his right hand back and forth like a pendulum. Rajam looked down and touched the gold pendant hanging from the chain around her neck. It was intact.

'If you don't come now, you will never wear your thali again.' Muthu was close to tears now. 'Arumugam annan is going to drink pesticide and kill himself.'

Selvi stifled a giggle. Rajam shrugged. Muthu looked at them in surprise.

'If that is what he wants to do, why stop him?' Selvi said, in a dismissive tone.

'How dare you say that? You call yourself his daughter?' He turned to Rajam. 'Did you hear what she said?'

'What do we lose? Let him do it.' Rajam's voice was calm and final.

Muthu was shocked, to say the least. He was hoping to make the family see sense and effect a reconciliation. It was to be the headline of next week's district circular: *Councillor Muthu saves family from dire fate*. What was he supposed to do now? Well, he wasn't going to give up so easily. He briskly walked back towards the centre of action.

A few moments later, Selvi received a call from her husband and Rajam from her sisters, all demanding the same thing. That they go immediately and rescue Arumugam who was on the verge of consuming poison. At any cost. Selvi asked Rajam to turn off her phone and did the same with hers. A delegation of older citizens came knocking on the door soon after and they too left empty-handed. 'Such cruel women. What an unlucky chap that Arumugam is!' they murmured as they went out of sight.

A cruel family! But, Selvi thought, they chose not to remember how the family turned cruel. They weren't around to pontificate on cruelty when Arumugam beat his wife every night. It got worse when he was fired for drinking on the job. He was home most of the time and he started harassing Selvi too. She had stopped speaking altogether, when finally Rajam decided not to take it any more and move back to Ayyanarpatti. It took two years before she would speak a full sentence again. But it did not end with that, of course. He followed them to the village a few years later, contrite and ready to reform his ways. It did not last the month. Thankfully, by then, Selvi was strong enough to pare off his blows. The beating stopped, but he still stole money, came home drunk, and woke the neighbourhood in the middle of the night with his shouting. Lately, he'd taken to frightening his grandchildren. Little Amuda, Selvi's three-year-old, had nightmares every night, thanks to her loving grandfather who insisted on chatting with her every evening. An unlucky chap indeed!

Meanwhile, back on Upper Street, Arumugam was showing no signs of giving in. He was standing on top of a mound next to the tea stall, holding up the pesticide can as if it were a sword. Closest to him were Chandran and Muthu, and a number of other men pleading with him to hand the can over to them. The women were standing to one side, hands over their lips, silent for the most part. The outer circle comprised of children who were tugging at their parents' shirts and saris; for them this spectacle was no substitute for real firecrackers.

'Anna, throw that bottle away. Whatever be the problem, just tell me and I'll fix it,' Muthu urged Arumugam.

'What will you fix? My family is not even here to see me dying.' Arumugam paused to take a swig out of the can. A collective gasp went up in the crowd.

'Which of you is brave enough to commit suicide? Here is a lesson for all of you – if you get no respect, there's no reason to live.' He lifted the can again.

'No, no,' they all cried.

He stopped. 'Nobody respects me in this village. No one cares.'

'We all care about you. In fact, I am so worried that I asked for a taxi in case something untoward happens. Look, the car is here now,' Muthu said.

The crowd turned towards where Muthu was pointing to see an old white Ambassador slowly make its way down the street. By the time they turned back towards Arumugam, the can was nearly empty. He laughed and flung it on the ground. The pungent smell of pesticide filled the air. Muthu rushed towards Arumugam, who fell down on the ground, unconscious.

~

Deepavali was a popular day for accidents, and it was a while before the hospital would admit Arumugam. Muthu's supposed political clout did not come to all that much use. They had to wait for hours before a doctor tended to the patient, and admitted him to the general ward. He was stable at the moment, but they were going to perform a barrage of tests the following day, the doctor said before leaving. They would have to wait for the test results before any diagnosis could be made. Muthu and Chandran thanked the doctor, and headed back to Ayyanarpatti.

By late evening, everyone in the village knew that Arumugam was on his deathbed.

'There was nothing more that could be done, the doctor said. Inform the family.'

'Look at how painfully you die if you have an ungrateful family,' they said, clustered around their verandas and kitchens.

'Selvi did not even want to go see him at the hospital. Is she really his daughter?'

'There was talk of another man in Rajam's life before she came back to the village,' someone whispered.

'Poor Muthu had, in fact, offered to take Arumugam to a private hospital in Trichy, where he would've got better treatment, but Selvi flatly refused.'

'And that hard-hearted woman who's going to be a widow soon – doesn't she have any shame?'

Ayyanarpatti went to bed, indignant.

~

Arumugam woke up early the next morning, feeling absolutely famished. He looked around, and was surprised to see he was in what looked like a hospital. He remembered drinking from a pesticide can, but otherwise his memory failed him. A nurse passed by, and he asked her for food, but she glared at him and went on her way. She had done enough for him; he had vomited a few times during the night. He looked in his pocket to see if he had any money. Fifteen rupees. More than enough for the bus back home. He waited for the nurse to leave the ward, and quietly sneaked out. By the time Selvi turned up at the hospital to check on her father, Arumugam was well on his way home.

The sound of firecrackers split the air as he alighted from the bus. Under cover of the excitement the previous day, Nithya had managed to go to town and bring back a load of crackers, which she had then sold off with a comfortable mark-up. The kids were told to go easy on the crackers because of an imminent death, but of course that only served to increase their frenzy. They wanted to burst everything they had bought before news reached the village. They knew they wouldn't be allowed to once the village went into mourning.

A 2000-wala exploded into a thousand-odd pieces, just as Arumugam walked into Upper Street. Preparations were on to light the next set when Arumugam walked slowly towards them through the smoky wake of the mala-wala.

'The ghost is here!' they shrieked and ran home shouting.

Arumugam was puzzled. Why were they running away from him? He wasn't drunk, not yet anyway. As he was pondering this, Muthu came out of his house running, and fell at his feet. Arumugam looked down at him, thoroughly confounded.

'Anna, you are alive! I knew you would be fine,' he said as he got up, and embraced Arumugam.

Soon, the rest of the village came out in droves to see the man who had returned from Yama's door.

'Is it really him? They say when someone is so close to death, he visits places dear to him. You don't think...?'

'Shh! It is him. He's come back from the dead.'

'Miracle!' they cried. 'He is walking! He must have been blessed by Kamakshi Amman herself!'

Everyone inquired after him, and invited he-who-had-been-blessed into their homes. Arumugam was initially bewildered at the reception, but with characteristic opportunism, he made the most of it. The next couple of days passed in a haze. There was no shortage of food and drink, or houses to stay in. He went to the Kamakshi temple every evening so that they could all be blessed by the goddess in his presence. He didn't even think about home until a week or so later, when it started dawning on him that the villagers were slowly losing interest in he-who-had-come-back-from-the-dead. He made some inquiries, and waited another day or two before he set foot on his doorstep, just to be safe. No one spoke a word to him, but the plate of food was waiting in the kitchen, as always. The mat on the veranda was all his too.

Possessed

Kaakka kaakka kanakavel kaakka
Nokka nokka nodiyil nokka
Thakka thakka thadaiyarai thakka…

Hamsa laughed at his friend. 'Mariamma is not afraid of your Murugan. You can chant all you want, but Murugan's golden spear isn't going to rescue you from her,' he said.

'Will your Allah help me then?' Mani asked, his voice cracking. 'Teach me a few Allah songs, please.'

Mani and Hamsa were on the way home from their primary school in Rayavaram town. They were identically dressed in khaki shorts, shirts that were once white, and rubber flip-flops. There was no question as to their religious affiliations – Hamsa had on his head a white skullcap, while traces of holy ash smeared early that morning could still be seen on Mani's forehead. Hamsa carried his books in his hand, while Mani's were in a yellow cloth bag that dangled from his right shoulder. They walked in the middle of the recently paved Karaikudi main road, since, other than for bus no. 22 and the occasional bullock cart, there was hardly any vehicular traffic on this stretch. They were nearing Sengeerai village, where Hamsa would say goodbye. Mani would then have to cross the forest to get home to Ayyanarpatti.

'Allah cannot help either, not with this Mariamma business. You have to be careful not to get caught.' Hamsa did not intend to scare his best friend but he wanted to ensure that Mani was properly warned of the danger ahead.

'I don't want to go home.' Mani's courage, whatever was left of it, was failing him.

'You can stay in my house tonight if you want,' Hamsa offered.

'I wish I could, but I can't. I'll have to deal with my father's cane if I don't get back home tonight. It's my turn to help with the ploughing tomorrow.'

'So you decide between your father and Mariamma!'

'I am not scared.' Mani tried to put on a brave front. 'Our maths teacher said there is no aazhamarathu Mariamma; we shouldn't believe in ghosts as that's just another superstition.'

'What does he know?' Maths was not Hamsa's favourite subject, so naturally the teacher was suspect too. 'He's not from here, is he? You better get home before it gets too late.'

Mani nodded. There was no point in delaying the inevitable. 'Come with me to the yeri bank, Hamsa.'

'Why do you want me to come with you? Your favourite maths teacher said there is no Mariamma! Go without fear!'

They could see the yeri embankment from where they were standing. It was just a few hundred yards away. Mani started running towards the bank without looking back.

'Mani!' Hamsa called out. He was now feeling sorry for

poor Mani. 'You are safe on this side of the forest. I'll wait here until you climb up the bank.'

Mani slowed down. Hamsa was right, of course. There was no point in running to the embankment as he needed his energy for what came after the yeri. Until the yeri, it was all barren flat land, where Hamsa could easily see him. Mariamma wouldn't dare to come here out in the open.

A few minutes later, he reached the foot of the embankment and started climbing up. The reservoir was not large but it was full and overflowing as a result of monsoon rains. A good year, his father had said. A good year meant that the Pongal festival would last longer. It also meant a new khaki half-trouser. He wouldn't have to make do with Neru's old shorts and use his waistband as a belt to keep it from sliding down his waist. Mani turned around once he reached the top. He could see Hamsa just off the main road, a speck in the distance. He waved. Hamsa waved back and turned towards his home in Sengeerai.

Mani tried to calm himself before he entered the forest. He came this way every day. Mariamma knew him, and she would not hurt him. His grandmother had told him that when she was alive Mariamma used to sing him lullabies. But Mani did not remember her. She drowned before he turned two: she jumped into the village well that the government had just built, and now her restless soul wandered all over the forest. Her favourite haunt was the aazhamaram, a banyan tree at the edge of the forest, where she came to rest every night. Every day, Mani had to cross Mariamma's banyan tree twice, on his way to school and back. However, until this fateful day, he had never had to cross the forest on his own.

He had stayed back in school rehearsing for the School Day play about an ancient Greek hero, a philosopher, condemned to consume poison for the crime of asking questions. Mani had the part of the prison guard who hands Socrates the cup of hemlock.

'I don't want to give anyone any poison,' he decided. He was now at the far end of the embankment where the forest began. He started walking slowly through the shrubs.

'Mariamma, please leave me alone,' he said, and promptly started at the sound of his own voice. But any sound was better than the deathly stillness that had taken over this edge of the forest. So he continued: *'You have suffered so much for the sake of this country, you have been driven out like a stray dog by your own countrymen, you...you...asked us...'*

He had forgotten the rest of the prison guard's lines. Perhaps he should recite something else, a poem that would keep out fear.

Achamillai achamillai achamenbathilaiye
Uchimeedhu van idindhu veezhukindra podhinum
Achamillai achamillai achamenbathilaiye

But wait, he thought. What did Subramania Bharathi of Ettayapuram town know about Ayyanarpatti's Mariamma? The famed Poet Laureate never walked in this dense forest, did he now? How would he know the ghosts of Mani's little village? Mani started walking faster. The shrubs were giving way to taller, denser trees, and he was soon in the middle of the forest. Usually, he and his friends would be looking out for peacocks and monkeys, but they didn't interest him now. All he wanted was to cross the banyan tree before it turned dark. He looked up at the sky. The sun seemed to be going down faster than usual now, and a westerly wind was blowing.

Only one thing could get him through the forest, Mani decided, the one thing he knew better than anyone else in his class. He meant to start in a loud voice but it came out in a whisper.

O rendu
Ee rendu naalu
Muvi rendu aaru
Naal rendu ettu

His plan was to go up to sixteen times sixteen, by which point he should be safely past the dreaded tree, and well into the outskirts of his village. Once he caught sight of the lonely Pillayar under the peepul tree, he had nothing to worry about, as the god would take care of him. If Pillayar did not oblige, Mani knew he could count on non-divine interventions – he'd be able to see the hurricane lanterns of his house from the peepul tree. All he had to do now was finish his multiplication tables. It was that simple, he told himself.

Mani was at eleven when he crossed the banyan tree. It looked like any other tree but he wasn't taking any chances. His eyes were glued to the trail in front of him and he dared not look up. Twelve. He should be able to see the Pillayar temple any second now.

'Twelve times twelve is one hundred and forty-four…'

Pillayar's peepul tree came into view. His spirits soared and he started running. Straight west, in front of him, the sun was about to go down completely. In another minute, it would be pitch-dark.

'Thirteen. Now for thirteen!'

But he couldn't, even though he knew the tables perfectly well. Now that he knew he was safe, he felt an intense desire to see Mariamma. At sundown, they said, she would be at the banyan tree, come what may. If he turned around now, the tree would be directly in his line of vision. Mani stopped and slowly turned around.

In the twilight, he saw a formless white translucence at the topmost branch of the banyan. As he watched transfixed, it morphed to take the form of a woman wearing a milk-white sari. He stood rooted to the spot. He could see her face now, the eyes glaring directly at him. Her lips started moving.

'Mani,' Mariamma whispered.

Mani dropped his school bag, and ran.

~

The next day, Mani's father sent out an urgent summons for the Samy. Mani had fever and, worse, he hadn't spoken a word since he returned home from school the day before. He was a boy possessed. The Samy specialized in exorcism, and only he'd be able to help Mani. People from all over the district called on him to exorcize ghosts, demons and fallen gods.

The Samy duly arrived in Ayyanarpatti that afternoon amid some fanfare. His bicycle was parked a furlong away, and he entered the village on foot. The Samy always walked the last furlong. He wore a flowing saffron robe that had not been washed in months. His hair was long and matted, and he had on a number of bead necklaces. In his hand, he held a wooden staff that doubled as his walking stick. He was alone when he turned into the village, but by the time he reached Mani's house he was at the head of a procession of children, drunks and old women. A couple of boys were dispatched to the fields to fetch the farm workers – nobody wanted to miss the spectacle they knew was coming.

Mani's father welcomed the Samy, and offered him buttermilk. Mani's mother was beside herself.

'I don't know what he has seen, Samy. But he has been like this since last night. His body is very hot. None of the leaves have had any effect. The fever is not coming down,' she explained.

'Has he eaten anything since last night?' the Samy inquired.

'No, he refuses to eat anything.'

The Samy turned to Mani, who was curled up in a fetal position on the mattress. He touched Mani's forehead.

'Mani, thambi, what did you see?' he asked the boy, frowning.

Mani shivered. He did not remember what he had seen. Whatever it was, he was sure he was never going to school again. He would never cross the forest; he had decided that he would not give in even if his maths teacher came home in person and asked him to return to school.

'What time did this incident occur?' the Samy asked Mani's mother.

'Late in the evening. He came back home just as the sun was setting.'

The Samy sat down on the floor cross-legged, and closed his eyes. He seemed to be absorbed deep in thought. Once assured of appropriate attention from everyone in the room, he spoke again.

'It could be any one. There are a few who have been doing the rounds recently. Just last week one of them caught hold of Karuppiah's son.'

'Yes, we heard about that. Please do something for our son too,' Mani's mother pleaded.

'Don't worry! We'll get to the bottom of this soon enough. Get neem leaves and incense, and bring him to the courtyard.'

'It's all ready, Samy,' said Mani's father. He lifted Mani from the mat, and carried him to the courtyard. Anticipating the event, Mani's aunt had already lit a small fire in the middle of the open yard. Neru, Mani's brother, was throwing twigs into the fire. When he saw his father carrying Mani in, he scampered off to tell everyone that the action was about to begin.

On one side of the fire, facing east, a mat was laid out, bordered by freshly cut neem leaves. Mani's father put him down gently on the mat. Mani could barely sit up. His father sat down beside him to support him. A pot of water, camphor and incense, and a plate full of holy ash were placed on the other side of the fire.

The Samy stood facing Mani and began chanting in a low voice; it was difficult to make out the words, or even the language. Mani's mother stood next to the Samy, her eyes closed in prayer. Soon, onlookers started gathering in the courtyard. A few kids climbed on the wall to get a better view of the proceedings. Neru leaned against the nearest pillar.

The Samy gathered some neem leaves in his hand, and walked clockwise around the fire and Mani a few times.

'Mani, who did you see yesterday?' he asked loudly.

'I don't remember,' Mani answered, his voice feeble.

'That's not my son. He does not sound like that,' his mother cried, opening her eyes.

'Shh! This is your son. Nobody's inside him. You be quiet, woman,' the Samy admonished her. He continued walking around the fire, chanting. There was no other sound for a few minutes.

Suddenly, Mani's mother let out a loud cry. All eyes turned towards her. Her hair had come loose and her eyes were bloodshot. She bent down, picked up the neem twigs by her feet and walked towards her son.

'Who are you?' she roared. 'Why did you get hold of my son? What do you want with him?' Her voice was very unlike her own.

Mani looked up at his mother. 'Amma…'

'Don't try to trick me, where is my son? Bring him back,' she cried, hitting Mani's head with the neem leaves in her hand. Mani started sobbing. The Samy walked swiftly towards the woman. He grabbed her hand, and pulled her away from her son.

'You know, don't you?' the Samy asked her, holding on to her arm. 'You know who frightened him. Tell me now!'

'I don't,' Mani's mother said as she struggled to be free.

'Yes, you do! I know you can talk to Maadan. Ask him who frightened your son.'

Mani's mother did not reply. The Samy picked up some camphor with his free hand and threw it into the fire. The courtyard was now thick with smoke. He picked up a few neem twigs and slapped her with them.

'Tell me who scared him. I will not let you go unless you tell me!' the Samy said and picked up his staff and raised it up in the air.

Mani's mother glared at the Samy for a few moments. Her head started moving round in circles.

'Karuppan, no, it's not Karuppan!'

'I know it's not Karuppan,' said the Samy as he brought the staff swiftly down on her shoulder.

'No, no, don't hit me. I know who she is!' she cried.

'Tell us then,' the Samy ordered her. He had expected this to go on for longer, but it looked like the onlookers would be disappointed.

'It is she who fell down the well.'

'Mariamma!' someone in the audience cried out.

Mani looked up instantly. He got up from his mat and cried out, 'No, I did not see anything. I did not see her!'

The Samy turned towards Mani and hugged him tightly. 'Sit down, boy! We know what to do. We have her.'

The boy sat down.

The Samy then turned to look at his mother. 'Calm down, woman! Your son will be all right,' he said, and beat her a few more times with neem leaves for good measure. She fainted, her task accomplished; Mani's aunt and a couple of other women came forward and dragged her away from the courtyard.

The Samy sat down across from Mani. From his waistband, he pulled out a long, thick, black thread. He dipped it in ash, and brought it to his eyes. 'Mani, show me your hand,' he said, his eyes still closed.

'Nobody will harm you now,' he said as he pulled Mani's right hand towards him. 'No one will dare touch you as long as this thread is on your wrist.' He tied it tight around Mani's wrist, making him wince. The Samy then took a handful of ash, and smeared it on Mani's face and chest. He turned to Mani's father.

'Go to the Pillayar temple tomorrow with nine coconuts. It is He who saved your son's life yesterday, and He will be Mani's guardian from now on. With Him and this sacred thread to protect him, even the Devil of Three Forests cannot do anything to your son.'

Mani's fever went down that night. A week later, he returned to school. He did not think of aazhamarathu Mariamma again that year. She did come back to him at the beginning of the next year but by then a new road had been laid from Ayyanarpatti to the embankment and he did not have to walk through the forest. Mani walked on this new road for a few months, until the following Pongal, when his father gifted him his old bicycle. He was free of the forest.

~

But what has all this ancient history to do with the Ayyanarpatti of our times? Dense forests, ghosts on banyan trees, villages far away from anywhere – doesn't all this belong to a previous century? Today, there are buses every fifteen minutes that will take you into town. If they did not run on time, taxis can be summoned. There is hardly any house left without a television set. Yes, they get all the five hundred and thirty-three channels that we get in the cities. Mobile phones, pre-loaded with Skype, are everywhere. A couple of the boys even have computers, and laptops with wireless connectivity. Only the very oldest of houses on Upper Street have tiled roofs and even those have indoor plumbing. The electricity is not very reliable but don't we have planned load shedding in the cities? Our modern village surely deserves to be featured in a modern story, not a rehashed period drama, but a story that reflects the times we live in.

Let's get to the story of our times then. We find ourselves once again on the main road from Rayavaram town. Neru and Mani, adult versions, were returning to Ayyanarpatti on Neru's motorcycle. Mani had gone to town to visit a few old school friends and Neru offered him a ride back as he had some work in the village. It was a blustery Karthigai evening, and the wind was out in full force. Just before they reached Sengeerai, Neru made a sharp left turn. He was going to take a short cut through the embankment.

'The yeri is overflowing. I haven't seen it full in a long time.'

'What?' Neru could hardly hear Mani over the sound of the motorcycle.

'I said the yeri is full,' Mani shouted from the pillion seat.

'Oh yes! This is a good year. After three years of failed monsoons, it's a huge blessing.'

'Remember how we always used to have good monsoons when we were kids? Now they have cut down the forests, and planted eucalyptus in its place and here is the consequence – failing rains.'

'Eucalyptus is low maintenance and high yield,' Neru pointed out.

'But it's not sustainable. Nothing will ever grow in this soil again, and the rains will keep failing.'

Neru gave a short laugh. 'There are people still living here – that is sustenance. It's either this, or the construction sites of Singapore and Dubai. There is no other choice.'

'There's always a choice.' Mani could not quite believe his brother.

Neru knew Mani had a point, but he was getting a tad weary of his city brother. Lofty ideals, with no grounding in reality, he thought warily.

'That's easy to say when you don't live here. But enough of that! Let me show you something else. Look to your right. What do you see?'

Mani turned to look. The dense forest of his childhood was in the process of being cut down. Gone were the most common trees of the forest – the milky palai, the auspicious veera and the divine kurunthai. Waiting to be cut down were a few peepuls, banyans and assorted shrubs. As far back as he could remember, the forest had hardly had any lantanas. But now lantana, the queen weed of barren land, was everywhere.

'Neru, stop! Where is Mariamma's banyan tree?' Mani cried out.

'I had a feeling you'd miss it. They cut it down a couple of months ago.'

'How did Mariamma let it go?'

'A special ceremony was performed at the Durga temple before they cut the tree down. It was meant to appease Mariamma. I hope she finds another residence.'

'Ah, appeasement! Is there anyone left who cannot be appeased?' Mani inquired.

'Well, they wanted to cut down the peepul tree too but Pillayar saved it. Nobody dares to cut down Pillayar's tree and incur His wrath.'

'Even the gods are useful sometimes!'

'More than you think, thambi. Here we are,' Neru said as he turned the final bend into the village.

'What are all these people doing here?'

Mani hopped down before Neru could bring the motorcycle to a complete stop. A large crowd had gathered in front of their family home on Upper Street. A few of them turned around when they heard the motorcycle. One of the men hurried over to Mani.

'Good you are here. Muthu came to find you. Didn't you see him on your way?'

'No,' Neru replied. 'We took the yeri short cut. What's the matter?'

'Nothing to worry about,' the man said, patting Mani on his back. 'The Samy has it under control.'

'The Samy!' Mani looked up sharply. 'What is that quacksalver doing here?'

'Don't say things like that, thambi. Go inside. Everything will be all right.'

The crowd made way for the brothers to go in. Mani was beginning to get concerned.

An all-too-familiar scene greeted them in the courtyard. In the centre of the courtyard was a small fire. Neem leaves were scattered all over the yard. The old Samy with his long, matted hair and bead necklaces was pacing around the fire. Mani's mother was leaning against the wooden pillar, looking worried and impatient. The audience was waiting in anticipation. Mani sensed that the act was about to begin. Perhaps this time he should just sit back and enjoy the show. His attention shifted to the child who was the star in this particular episode of the exorcist.

She was sitting on the mat in front of the fire, shivering. Mani gasped.

'Kavitha!'

He felt his wife's hand on his shoulder.

'She saw something in the backyard and got scared. She has a fever now. I don't know what they are doing. They wouldn't listen to me!' His city-bred wife trying to make sense of the spectacle – this would be hilarious, if only it wasn't their daughter on the mat. He walked quickly to the centre of the courtyard and lifted his daughter.

'Appa,' cried Kavitha as she buried her head in his shoulder.

A collective gasp escaped from the audience.

'It's going to be all right, darling! Give me a blanket, someone,' Mani said.

The Samy was taken aback. 'Mani, what are you doing? Put the child down. We need to find out who got hold of her.'

'There's no need to do anything of the sort. I don't think your services are needed any more,' Mani said, trying hard to keep his voice calm.

'Mani, put her down now. If you don't, only Kali knows what will happen to her.'

'I know very well what'll happen to my child if I leave her at your mercy. I suggest you take off before I throw you out of the house.' Mani's attempt at self-control was laughably inadequate.

The spectators had not been expecting this. Still, no one came forward to reason with Mani. He was known to be headstrong, even bull-headed sometimes. A non-believer. Poor child, they murmured, she'll suffer the consequences.

Mani turned to take his daughter inside when he heard a loud snort. He should have known. It was only a question of time before this happened. His mother.

'Maadan is talking to me,' she cried as her hair came loose. 'I'll find out who it is!'

Mani walked up to her, still carrying his daughter. He spoke slowly. 'Tell me what Maadan's telling you. Look at me and tell me what Maadan is telling you.'

The old woman started breathing heavily. Her head started moving round in circles.

'Maadan,' she shouted. 'Yes, tell me! I am waiting.'

'Amma, look at me! I want you to look at me and talk to this Maadan of yours. Let us see if he still wants to talk to you.'

His mother lifted her head to gaze up at her son. She stared at him for a few moments before she came to the conclusion that it was of no use. He would not understand. She collapsed into the arms of the two women waiting behind her.

Mani did not see his mother again until much later that

night. She did not come up to the room to check on Kavitha when her temperature kept climbing steadily. His wife told him she was cloistered in a corner of the kitchen, refusing food and drink. And then it was three in the morning, and he was bundling Kavitha into her mother's lap, in the back seat of the Ambassador taxi they had summoned from town. Only then did he sense his mother behind the door. He ignored her, and climbed into the front of the car, next to the driver.

'I'll follow in the motorcycle,' Neru said. 'Don't worry,' he touched his brother's shoulder. 'This pediatrician is good. Kavi will be fine.'

As the driver reversed the car, Mani finally brought himself to look at the old woman sulking behind the door. She looked grim, but was glaring at him triumphantly. He averted his eyes. The car sped through the night to Rayavaram town.

God's Own Country

Peepul tree no. 57 was missing.

Nithya jumped off her bicycle and checked the numbers painted on the trees to be sure. Fifty-four, fifty-five, fifty-six, fifty-eight. She was certain she had seen tree no. 57 the last time she passed by this stretch. Where could it have gone? Had the Moorthy brothers cut it down for their new timber depot? These trees were officially protected and hence the numbering, but that meant nothing. Whole mountains had disappeared over on the Madurai road, courtesy of the granite mafia. What is one poor peepul tree beside a mountain? Perhaps during the next tree census someone would file a missing tree FIR at the town police station.

PEEPUL TREE NO. 57 ON THE TRICHY-KARAIKUDI HIGHWAY IS MISSING, SIR. IT WAS DEFINITELY PRESENT IN THE LAST CENSUS. FIFTEEN YEARS AGO, SIR. I AGREE IT COULDN'T HAVE RUN AWAY, SIR. NO SIR, I HAVE NOT CHECKED WITH ITS NEIGHBOURS WHEN IT WAS LAST SEEN. SHOULD I GO AND ASK RIGHT NOW, SIR?

She laughed out loud at the unfortunate census official's plight as she turned off the highway and on to the road to Ayyanarpatti. She was still laughing when the grey Toyota Innova overtook her. A Madurai registration – it wasn't a number she recognized, and she knew all those that ever came this way. She pedalled faster, but it proved unnecessary. The brake lights came on, and in a couple of minutes, her bicycle was alongside the car.

The man in the front passenger seat leaned out. Sallow face, big moustache.

'Sister,' he addressed Nithya, 'do you know where the old corn field is?'

Definitely a Madurai accent.

'Old corn field?' Nithya did not know of a corn field in these parts. She had heard stories of stolen corn from her grandmother but she had never seen corn grown in the village fields.

'Yes, where the college is going to be built.'

'Ah, yes.' Everyone knew the college site. 'If you go straight until the second banyan tree, and then take a left and go down for a few minutes, you'll be there. You will see a workers' shed, you can't miss it,' she answered.

'Thanks, sister.'

'But you can't take the car all the way, there's no road. You'll have to get out at the banyan tree, and walk the rest of the way.'

'That's all right.' The head went inside. The car sped away.

Nithya's curiosity was piqued. What business did these strangers have in the abandoned college site? It was just a large tract of barren land that was part of Rathinam's property, but nobody in his family did much with it. It could have been an old corn field, she supposed. Were these men planning to sow corn in Rathinam's land? That sounded unlikely.

She caught up with the car again at the second banyan tree. The driver was sitting inside. The two passengers had alighted, however, and were looking towards the dilapidated shed. They looked so much alike that Nithya decided they must be brothers. They were both tall, fair and clean-shaven, with sandalwood paste on their foreheads and identical gold bracelets – city types, all right. She looked down at the edges of their spotless white dhotis to confirm her suspicions – yes, coloured borders signifying their political affiliation. Well, why not? Their party was in power at the state level, and the sitting MP for the constituency belonged to their party as well.

'I'm going that way, I can show you the old corn field,' she offered.

No one answered for a few seconds. 'No, that's all right. We are waiting for someone...Isn't it time you got back home?' The man who'd asked her for directions frowned disapprovingly.

Nithya sighed and got back on her bicycle without a word. She was in no mood to hear another 'girls of nowadays' tirade from city folk, especially ones with ostensible political connections. The farther you stayed away from them, the better.

'Why don't you call Muthu? Didn't he say he'd be here at 5.30?'

Her curiosity got the better of her. 'Muthu, the councillor? Are you Muthu's friends?'

'Yes, he was supposed to meet us here,' one of the men answered reluctantly.

'Oh, really?' she could not hide her surprise this time.

'It's nothing,' his brother volunteered. 'He's just showing us his lands. We are from Madurai city and have not seen a lot of villages.'

'But these are not Muthu's lands.' This was beginning to sound stranger and stranger.

'We know,' the man answered. 'We just wanted to look at village lands to get an idea.'

She wasn't going to get much out of these men. 'I'll be off. If I see Muthu on the way, I'll tell him you are waiting here.'

By the time she reached the village, the sun was well on its way down and it was noticeably cooler. She looked at her phone – hardly 6 o' clock. The month of Markazhi might have arrived late in Ayyanarpatti but she seemed to be making up for it quite well. Nithya headed straight for Balu's tea shop. A hot tea and vadai in this weather would be heavenly. Moreover, Balu usually knew everything that went on in the village and would be happy to hear of any new happenings.

'Muthu's friends, you say?' Balu said thoughtfully, handing Nithya her free tea for bringing in hot news. 'They must be up to something.'

'But what could it be? They can't be looking to farm the land.'

Balu laughed. 'Of course not.'

'What about the college?'

'That's been dead in the water for a while now.'

'Do you think they are up to something illegal?'

'Why do you think that?'

'Why would they not tell me why they were here? They are hiding something.'

'Hmm. I guess that's true.'

'What illegal business are you thinking of?'

'Illicit liquor?'

'There's no money in that these days now that the government has taken over the business of selling alcohol and there's a TASMAC shop around every corner. Muthu will be looking at bigger fish.'

'What could it be then? You don't suppose women are involved, do you?'

'Nithya, what nonsense you talk! A grown-up girl talking like this! You watch too many films. You ought to be ashamed of yourself.'

'Well, what else could it be then?'

Balu had to admit he was stumped. 'Let's keep an eye out and see what happens.'

'Okay. Let me know if you hear anything,' said Nithya and took her leave.

Before long, the whole village had heard about Muthu and his friends visiting the abandoned site outside the village. The 'college site' had some history to it. A few years ago, as engineering colleges sprang up in every nook and corner of the state in an effort to capitalize on our country's aspiration to become the back office of the world, two of Rathinam's business associates who ran a transportation business in town had approached him with a view to build an engineering college in his land. The men wanted to expand beyond buses and trucks, and higher education, they had gathered, was a lucrative business. This was the time when real estate in the cities was starting to boom considerably and hence it was better to set the institution far away from the urban centres. This also had the added advantage of being able to cater to the aspirational rural populace and, in this particular case, it was also a logical expansion for the existing business as students will need to be transported to and from the college. Rathinam had gladly acquiesced, his only request being that the college be named after his family. With much fanfare, the foundation stone was laid and a shed constructed to house the workers and equipment. But alas, a series of unrelated unfortunate events followed – mounting losses in the transportation business, a glut of professional colleges in the region, the wider economic meltdown followed by a fall in student demand – and as a result, the plan had to be shelved for a while. There was then a delayed realization that the real money was in medical colleges – nearly a crore per admission as opposed to just a few lakh for an engineering seat – but it also meant that a proportional amount had to be paid to political coffers to acquire the necessary permits for a medical institution. There was a change of guard at the state level during this time and as a result the price for permission went up exponentially, which proved to be the final nail in the coffin for the project. For years now, the college was all but forgotten, the lonely shed in the parched land being the only sign of the stalled development.

In the first few years, there used to be talk of renewed

interest once every few months – the college work will begin, a new layout is being planned – but after a while, the villagers became wise to the rumours. But now, it was different. Not only had Nithya seen the visitors again a few days later, traipsing around the land with ropes and measuring tape in hand but this time it was well known that Councillor Muthu was also involved. His star, it was said, was in the ascendant in the district. All sorts of new rumours were in circulation. The popular view was that Muthu was slowly encroaching on Rathinam's lands, and soon he would take over them and build a shopping mall. Another claimed that he was going to build a party office in the usurped land. A third, which Nithya played a minor role in starting, stated that he was going to start a new political party, and an astrologer had suggested that the party headquarters should be built at the abandoned college site.

When someone asked Muthu what he was up to, he was secretive and pompous as usual: 'Be patient. All shall be revealed in due course.'

These rumours reached Rathinam's ears within the day. Rathinam was bemused, to say the least. The site was, needless to say, a touchy subject for him and for years he had harboured the hope that an institution bearing his name would be built on it. But not any more, not when his old business partners had to sell their trucks and property, and live in rented accommodation. There was no hope any more. But Muthu, what was he up to? He could not have plans for his land without consulting him, could he now? He decided to wait for Muthu to come to him. He had known Muthu since he was a little boy. A good-for-nothing fellow who lived off the money his brother sends from Singapore. Not a bad sort though, he told himself, just had too many delusions of grandeur which wasn't uncommon in the youth of our day.

A week later, Muthu rang up Rathinam and requested him to come to the party office in town. Rathinam refused. He would not go to the office of any political party. Muthu reluctantly agreed to drop by Rathinam's place that evening.

A few minutes before Muthu arrived, Nithya put in an appearance at Rathinam's house. She made up a story about borrowing a book from Rathinam's niece who was conveniently not at home. She was determined to find out what was going on especially if Muthu was involved. Nithya and Muthu had grown up in adjacent houses on Upper Street and there was no love lost between them. Soon Muthu arrived on the scene.

'Rathinam anna, we haven't met in so many months. Have you been out of town?' he enquired respectfully.

'No, I've been here all the time. You are the busy one. You don't have time for us any more,' Rathinam answered.

'How can you say that? I always think of you, you know that. With your blessings only, I live!' Muthu was vehement.

'Otherwise you'd have jumped into the government well long ago and committed suicide,' Nithya sympathized with Muthu.

Muthu turned pale. He looked around to see Nithya grinning at him. 'What are you doing here?'

'Let her be, Muthu. How is Mari?' Rathinam asked Muthu.

'He's doing well in Singapore. Sometimes I think I should

also go to Singapore and be like him. Life is very good there.'

'Why don't you go then?'

'Who'll look after everything at home, anna? Nowadays, there's also a lot of party work – someone has to work for our country. If my back is turned for a minute, someone will stab me.'

'That is how politics is played, isn't it? It's not very easy, I know.'

'No, it's not. But I'm seeing the light now. If all goes according to plan, I think I can swing a seat.'

'For the regional election? I hope you get it, we'll vote for you.'

Muthu laughed. 'Who cares about regional elections? I am thinking bigger, much bigger.'

'You mean the MLA seat?' Rathinam sounded surprised.

'No, mama, he is going to be the new prime minister. Haven't you heard?' Nithya again.

'You shouldn't let her inside your house. She's nothing but trouble!' Muthu was indignant.

Rathinam ignored him. 'A number of people are vying for the seat, people with a lot of influence and money. How are you planning to secure it?'

'Nowadays I have value at the top. Even last week when I was in Chennai, I was called in to a special meeting with the leader.'

'I see,' Rathinam frowned and came to the subject at hand. 'What did you want to see me about?'

'I was just coming to that. But I will not speak further if she is here.' He lowered his voice. 'This is important business.'

Rathinam looked at both of them in exasperation. Nithya

slowly rose up and left the room, she knew there was no point in putting up a fight. She was about to plonk down under the window outside the room when Muthu stepped out to glare at her. She promptly left the house; she would have to think of another way to get to the bottom of this.

Luckily for Nithya, she didn't have to wait long. Her mother mentioned in passing the next morning that Neru, her lawyer periappa who lived in town, was expected that evening for tea. He was coming to meet Rathinam, she said. It made perfect sense to Nithya. Neru was usually consulted by the villagers on all sorts of business transactions and if Rathinam had summoned Neru, it had to do with Muthu's plan, she reasoned. The evening found her again at Rathinam's house with another excuse.

'Neru, come on in. A lot of confusion – I have no idea what do.' Rathinam invited Neru inside.

'Tell me about it...Nithya, what are you doing here? Don't you have to study?' Neru asked his niece. He knew she was rather inquisitive.

'My exams are over. I am just returning some books,' she mumbled but made no effort to leave the scene.

'This time it is a school, Neru! I don't know what to do,' Rathinam blurted out.

'A school? We already have a child care centre and a primary school in the village. Even those are not filled to capacity because most people send their children to the English medium school in town. What is the need for a new school?' Neru was truly surprised. He had expected Muthu and his pals to come up with an half-baked idea for a factory or a warehouse, but a school?

'That is what I thought but this school is different. They want to start an international school in the land.'

'Who are they?'

Neru was amused. Even by Muthu's standards, this was not making sense. Nithya listened quietly, it was better not to advertise her presence any more than necessary.

'Muthu's friends from Madurai, they already own a number of schools in Madurai district which are very famous. They are from a renowned family and well-regarded, he said. Nithya saw them the other day at the site.'

'Nithya, I have no idea why you're going around deserted places meeting strangers from God knows where. There is no safety—' Neru began.

'I was coming back from town after my exams. Would you rather I not go to college?' she demanded.

Neru did not reply. He would have to have this conversation with her later.

'Muthu said the people he is working with have a deep interest in education, not like the transport guys who were just in it for the money. A lot of rich people send their children to these schools which will have facilities at the international level like tennis courts and air-conditioned classrooms,' Rathinam continued.

Nithya was starting to feel jealous. There were no A/C classrooms in her college; the computer lab had A/C in name only and now, kids would have cool classrooms! Life wasn't fair.

'How much is the donation and fees?'

'It will be very high but these schools are very much in demand now. Business people send their children to these only nowadays; nobody goes to matriculation or state board schools. It is not like regular schools where English medium is in name only, he said. Everyone speaks English all the time.'

'I see but I don't think we have that many business people in the district who can afford the fees,' said Neru, dryly. 'I am afraid this sounds like the engineering college story all over again. I wouldn't go ahead if I were you, Rathinam.'

'But they want to buy the land Neru.'

'What? They want to buy it outright?'

'Yes, at a lower price than I'd want to sell but it is not a bad price with the market being what it is.'

'Are you certain?'

'Yes. Muthu was clear about that.'

'He will probably get some commission then. Hmm. In that case, Rathinam, get your money first and sell it. The land has been lying barren for decades and this may be your best opportunity to get good money for it.'

'But this land has been in my family for generations. These people…we don't know who they are.'

'You just said they are from a renowned family. Meet them and decide but if they give you a good price, take it. I will have a chat with Muthu if you like.'

'Muthu said he has value at the top now. He was talking about an MLA ticket.'

'Nonsense. They are not fools to give a non-entity like Muthu an MLA ticket. On this land issue though, you will be fine as long as you are careful. Just get the best price and don't sign anything until all the money is paid.'

'I'll be careful,' said Rathinam and thanked Neru for his help.

In a few weeks, it was all settled. Rathinam and the men from Madurai haggled over the price with Muthu as the chief negotiator and finally settled on an amicable amount. It turned out that the buyers had consulted an astrologer who told them that the site was the best possible location to start the school, and therefore they were willing to pay more than what they had originally anticipated. The final amount changed hands, and an auspicious day in the month of Thai was reserved for laying the foundation stone for the future school. The day was deemed auspicious by the virtue of the fact that the MP for the constituency was visiting, and this was the only day that was free in his diary. Muthu was ecstatic. He was now very visible in the regional party organization as the MP was coming to his little village! The villagers could not believe their good luck. The MP was going to eat in their village and, soon, they would have an international school of their own where the children of who's who of the district will come to study.

Muthu took upon himself the task of supervising preparations for the MP visit. He recruited Chandran, Balu and a couple of others for a few days to help him with the preparations. He decided that there would be a special dance performance by primary school children after the foundation stone ceremony. The stage needed to be set up for the ceremony; loudspeakers and photographers needed to be arranged; garlands and shawls had to be bought. As this was the MP, they were likely to get media coverage. The regional cable channels – Sun, Jaya, Kalaignar and Vijay – would be there at the event. The older children who went to schools in the town were told not to go that day. A special chef was summoned from Kaanadukaathan to prepare food for the event.

As the preparations went on for the ceremony, Nithya was engaged in investigations of her own. The school business did not sit well with her – for one, Muthu was involved, so something had to be wrong, she told herself. Two, she and the rest of the populace were subjected to big posters of the future school all along the main road and if truth be told she was more than a little jealous that this posh school had not been around in her time. But she was out of ideas as to how to go about finding more when one day her aunt showed her the flyer she had picked up at a textile shop in town.

Nalandha International School, it said, is a new kind of school not seen in the region until then. The teachers were trained abroad, and the children would not only learn what is taught in America but they would also live the American life here in India. Admission was guaranteed in top tier colleges both in India and abroad. They were going to start with the primary years the following academic year and applications were invited from suitable parents. It was clearly spelt out that parents would be interviewed first before any admission decisions were taken. There was an address in fine print at the bottom, and Nithya's aunt wanted her to get an application form for her son Thiru.

'But athai, the cost is close to a lakh per month in these schools. I have been reading about them online.'

'Then you should know that they are also very exclusive and they provide the best education for the kids.'

'I asked Siva master about it and he thought this school is a joke and no one should send their children there.'

'What does Siva master know about international schools? He worked in the local school all his life. Muthu said everyone's been asking him about the school and there may not be enough places next year. He visited one of the schools run by the same management in Madurai and it was like being in America. Can you believe that?'

'When did he go to America?'

'Nithya, I am only asking you to get me an application form and find out more about the interview.'

'You can't be seriously thinking about this. We can't afford it.'

'Let me worry about that. Just go along and get me a form.'

'All right.' Nithya finally agreed. She knew her aunt wasn't the only one considering sending her children there. She owed it to the kids of Ayyanarpatti to find out if the school was worth it; she felt like she had their future in her hands.

And so the next day found Nithya and her friend Priya in front of a narrow three-storey building at one end of the town high street.

'Here is the plan,' Nithya whispered to Priya. 'If I don't come out in twenty minutes, you call me on my phone.'

'Why do you want to go in if you don't think it's safe?' Priya asked. 'Perhaps we should both go in together.'

'No, this is better as you can call me and, if needed, get help.'

'I thought this was a school office.'

'That's what it says but I don't trust them. Muthu is involved, remember?'

'All right, I will wait here,' Priya reluctantly agreed. Nithya entered the building and climbed up two flights of stairs. Once she reached the second floor, she looked around and there was a glass door engraved with the room number: 201 – Nalandha International School Office.

Nithya entered the anteroom to find a girl approximately her age sitting behind a table. There were posters of the school plastered on the wall behind her with pictures of happy children, all fair-skinned and smartly dressed, sitting in class listening attentively, or playing tennis in an immaculate grass court.

A school to help your child achieve his full potential.

The girl looked up at Nithya as if expecting her. 'You are late; Madam is waiting for you.'

'What?'

'You can go inside, Madam doesn't like people being late,' she continued, pointing at the door behind her leading on to an inner office. Nithya decided to play along though she had no idea why anyone was expecting her. She walked straight up to the door and knocked on it.

'Come in,' said a voice with steel in it.

Nithya gingerly walked in. She encountered a severe, well-dressed woman spouting a teacher bun peering at her suspiciously through her glasses.

'You're late.'

'The bus did not come on time.' Nithya said the first thing that came to her mind.

'The buses never come on time but that doesn't mean you can be late. How can I trust you to come to school on time?'

Ah, this teacher thought she was a prospective student. 'But I have finished school already.'

The woman glared at her. 'Do you think I hire teachers who haven't graduated from school?'

She was being interviewed for a teaching position!

'No ma'am,' Nithya said dutifully. She could play the part now that she knew who she was supposed to be. She just hoped the real interviewee did not show up until she was through.

'Can you speak English?'

'Yes ma'am.'

'Your application says you studied physics in college. You can teach science then?'

'Certainly ma'am. I am good at science but I am not very familiar with the syllabus.'

'What do you mean? It is the same that you learnt.'

'But this is an international school...'

'You say you are a physics major. Tell me, are the three laws of motion different in the international syllabus?'

'No ma'am.'

'Newton is from England, isn't he? The laws of motion are more valid internationally because of that. Why would we teach anything different?'

Nithya thought about this for a few seconds but could not find fault with this line of argument. 'I understand,' she said.

'In any case, the syllabus is ours only. It is an international school but we follow CBSE.'

'Then why is it an international school?'

'You need to learn to stop asking so many questions. The name has "international" in it because we follow international standards, not because of the syllabus.'

'I see. Ma'am, I read that the teachers receive training abroad.'

The woman laughed. 'Where did you read that? In a few years if you do well, we will see about that.'

'How many students will there be in the class, ma'am?'

'We are expecting fifty-five per class. Have you done any teacher training?'

'Not yet, ma'am.'

'That's okay. The management have a teacher training institute in Madurai that you will need to attend. It is a certificate course for eight weeks.'

'Okay ma'am. How many teachers are there?'

'We'll have enough. Do you have any friends who want to join? If so, ask them to contact me. They can do the training course.'

'I will tell them.'

'Leave your address and mobile number with the girl outside. We will be in touch regarding the course soon.'

'Ma'am…'

'What?'

'What about salary?'

'You should pay us for giving you a job. You will be paid enough but ask such questions and your salary will go down.'

'Sorry ma'am.' Nithya got up to leave.

'Not that I need to mention it but the dress code is strictly sari only; you can't wear anything else to school,' the woman said, looking Nithya up and down.

'Is that also international standards?' Now that she was about to leave, there was no further need for restraint.

'You think international means the right to teach in

school half-naked? I am not sure you are the right candidate for this school.'

'I agree.'

'What? Who sent you here again?'

Before Nithya could reply, two things happened simultaneously. The girl at reception opened the door, and she was standing with a demure girl dressed in a sari carrying an A4 folder. Nithya's phone started ringing insistently – Priya was getting anxious. Nithya vanished from the scene as fast as she could.

'What do you mean it is not really international?' Priya asked. The girls were on the bus back to the village. Nithya's mind was working overtime. She had to expose the school scam but how? No one would believe her.

'Just what I said. They just have a name to get money from people. They don't even have teachers. You and I can teach...wait.'

'What?'

'No. 72 is gone. It was here last week.'

'Huh?'

'Nothing. Never mind.' The beginnings of an idea had just crossed Nithya's mind. A one-shot plan to stop the school and the felling of peepul trees, not to mention the look on Muthu's face when he found out.

~

The day of the foundation stone ceremony finally arrived. The MP was late by a couple of hours, as expected. There was yet another last-minute change – as he was in a hurry, the MP would not be stopping at the village. He'd be at the school site for a few minutes and then on his way. Muthu was dejected but determined to make the best of it. When the MP's entourage arrived in a twelve-car convoy, he was the first one to reach the door and open it for the MP to step out. The men from Madurai garlanded the MP who was then led to the foundation stone. The MP took the pickaxe handed to him and posed for the cameras. Muthu was there right next to him in all the photos. The MP then opened the screen and displayed the granite stone to the world. His name was engraved in a font about five sizes larger than anyone else's.

After this, the MP was invited to the stage and a number of decorative shawls were wrapped around him. He was asked to speak a few inspiring words to the people of the village.

'My dear brothers and sisters, girls and boys…' he began.

TOCK! TOCK!

Muthu whirled around. Where was that sound coming from? What was that idiot Kuppan doing with the pickaxe right behind the stage? He looked for Balu but could not locate him.

'It gives me the greatest of pleasures to be with you today at the start of this noble venture, an international school in your village, the first in our district…'

'Ayyo!' TOCK!

Muthu turned again. The MP heard it too this time. He did not look happy.

'Our schools are our temples. This is where your children, the youth of today will be shaped and they will lead not just our state and our country but the whole…'

'PILLAYAR! PILLAYAR!'

It was Nithya. She was running towards the stage. 'Kuppan found a Pillayar. There's a Pillayar in the land.'

The crowd went wild. The Remover of Obstacles, the God of Beginnings, found in this land? They started running towards where Kuppan was digging.

'Hold on, hold on,' Muthu shouted to no avail. The MP glared at him. 'Let's go there,' Muthu said and led the MP to where the action had shifted.

'What is going on here?'

'We found a Pillayar samy in the land. Here,' said Nithya who was back at the foundation stone site where Kuppan was digging. She gingerly lifted a very muddy stone statue of the beloved elephant god up for everyone to see. A few of the villagers prostrated on the ground.

'How did the Pillayar get here?' someone asked.

'This is sacred land,' Nithya shouted. 'This is Pillayar's own land. He wanted to be found here.'

'Yes!' shouted the crowd as they cupped their hands and started praying.

Muthu saw his chance. He took the microphone from the MP and shouted. 'In this sacred land, on this blessed day, the honourable MP would like to say some words.' He thrust the microphone back at the MP.

'My dear brothers and sisters, I am extremely fortunate as is each and every one of you to be present on such an occasion. I cannot tell you how happy I am today. The Pillayar wanted to be discovered here in this holy land and we have found him. How blessed are we?'

'Very blessed!' the crowd shouted back.

'This land is holy land. The Pillayar does not like Pillayarpatti any more,' he said making a dismissive reference to the nearby town famous for being the home of Pillayar. 'He likes your little village and I think we should let him stay here. Pillayar's home is Ayyanarpatti from now on!'

'Long live Pillayar! Long live our MP!'

'We will build a Pillayar temple here to make Him happy and to ensure that he stays with us. He will look after us like He has done since the beginning of time.'

'Long live our MP!'

~

A few days later, once the dust settled down, Neru visited the village to have a chat with his niece who he was sure had played a not insignificant role in l'affaire du Pillayar.

'Nithya, how did the Pillayar get there?'

'He was there himself, periappa.'

'So you had nothing to do with it?'

'What do I have to do with his divinity?'

'Well, he wasn't found earlier when the college shed was built.'

'How would I know when he decides to appear? And anyway, where would I find a Pillayar statue that ancient? I would have to go to some old forgotten temple in some godforsaken forest and steal it!'

'No, you'd have to go up to our attic which has a lot of old idols. Did you have anything to do with it?'

'Not much. I'm glad it happened though. The school was a con job to grab money from unsuspecting people.'

'You don't know that.'

'I do. They tried to give me a job as a teacher. I know, you don't believe me but it happened.'

'But now the land will be barren and useless.'

'You are calling a temple useless?'

'What good is going to come of yet another temple?'

Nithya looked up at her uncle and wondered how much she should divulge. She said finally, 'Thousands of people will flock to our temple once it's built. It will be bigger than the Kamakshi temple.'

Neru looked at his niece in surprise. 'You seem to have thought this through,' he said.

'Look at how much money comes into the Tirupati coffers every year.'

'I hope you turn out to be right. Already we are in the news all over the country as the true home of Pillayar. Muthu has done a decent publicity job. If we become the Tirupati of Pillayar, that'll mean a lot of revenue.'

'Yes, we'll be the prosperous home of a very, very wealthy god! And you know what's even better?' Nithya giggled. 'The whole world knows Pillayar loves peepul trees, so they will be safe. No more missing peepul trees on Pillayar's highway.'

Peepul trees? Neru wasn't sure how they fit in but he did not probe further. Sometimes, it was better not to know.

A House on Upper Street

Ayyanarpatti is a one-street village. You wouldn't know this from looking at the map as you will see a number of branches diverging from the crescent-shaped artery that is Upper Street. But these side streets are inconsequential and not important enough to merit names except for perhaps the one leading to the Amman and Durga temples which the locals call Temple Way. Diagonally opposite to the temples, at the farthest point from them in the village, stand a dozen or so small thatched-roof huts, in front of one of which our story begins.

Kumar opened his eyes wide and looked up at the darkening skies – he had grown up with stories of hailstones during Thai and Pankuni but he had never once seen it happen. Not in Ayyanarpatti at any rate. The winters in St Paul, Minnesota, where he was due to go back soon did not count. After a few minutes, he gave up staring at the sky as his neck was beginning to ache, and reached for the phone lying next to him on the coir cot. He dialled the number for Kanaka aachi. No luck. He would have to go see her in person.

'Thambi…'

He heard his mother behind him. 'Yes?'

'Thangam will finish college soon. A few alliances have come informally, and it's time we took them seriously,' she began.

Kumar turned around on his side to look at her. She was in her late forties but looked much older. Her face was wrinkled, and her hair mostly grey. Premature ageing as a consequence of a lifetime of manual labour, but he knew she was as fit as a fiddle for someone her age.

'Amma, you finalize the alliance you think is best. We'll have a grand wedding and send her off with everything she deserves.'

'But how can we start looking seriously without a proper roof over our heads? How will they come to this hut?' His mother stretched out her palm at the two-room thatch they called home.

Kumar did not answer immediately. His mother wouldn't have said that a few years ago, then again a few years ago he was still in college on a scholarship. The circumstances were different. Now, he was a software engineer and they had the financial muscle to look at matches for his sister that they could not have dreamed of earlier. His mother was bang on: they needed a new house to attract a good match. They needed a structure made of real bricks, one which boasted more than two tiny rooms. He wondered if he should tell her his plans for the house but decided against it. All in good time. He would tell her once everything was settled.

'Don't worry about it, we'll have a new house before the wedding.'

'There's no reason why I should not do farm work. I am healthy. I will work for another year and save money,' his mother said hesitantly.

Kumar laughed. 'With the money you earn from farm work, you'll have to work for ten years to build a hut like this.'

'But how else…'

'I've told you not to worry about all this,' he said, a tad impatient. 'I am doing well in my work. Soon, I will take you to America and you will see for yourself.'

'But…'

'Amma, you are not going to do farm work again.' Kumar was firm. 'Forty years of tilling the fields to make money for the landlords is enough. I promise you that you will have a house – one that you have only dreamt of,' he reassured his mother.

'In that case, there is some land behind Kuppan's house. We can build there.'

'You focus on finding the perfect groom for Thangam and let me take care of the house. Agreed?'

His mother grinned. 'If that's your wish, so be it.'

'Good, that's settled.' Kumar stood up and walked towards his old bicycle parked in front of the house. 'I am going to town to meet some people. I'll be back at sundown.'

'Have tea before you go, thambi.'

'I'll have tea in town. I am already late,' said Kumar as he unlocked the bicycle and set off.

He rode past the old government well, now dry. The huts started disappearing as he crossed the well, and were replaced by one-storey concrete structures on his left. The right side of the unpaved road was taken up by animal sheds followed by haystacks and threshing grounds for the nearby paddy fields. Soon he reached Upper Street and the large houses of the traditional landowners came into view. He slowed down. He passed by the periya veedu, once the largest house in the village, and could not resist peeking into the barn. Only two cows there now. The bullock cart that was usually parked under the almond tree in front of the house was nowhere to be seen. When he was a boy, climbing on to the cart used to be the crowning ambition of his young life. He'd attempted to get on it several times but was always chased away. One new moon night, after everyone had fallen asleep, he'd braved the numerous ghosts of the village and come all the way to Upper Street to climb up the cart. It was the happiest occasion of his childhood.

He looked at his watch. It was the time of day when the labourers done with the day's work would wait outside the back entrance of the periya veedu. He clearly remembered standing near the household well with his mother, waiting for the food to come out of the kitchen. Hot porridge and spicy pickle would be served in pale aluminium plates for the farmhands and their children who happened to be around. He didn't eat on stainless steel plates until he moved to the city for his first job. They happened to be the first thing he bought with his first ever salary. One plate, two tumblers and two ladles in gleaming stainless steel.

He wondered if there were labourers at the rear entrance nowadays – probably not. Labour was hard to come by; no one needed the money as the boys were sending in dollars earned from the construction sites of Singapore and the Middle East.

'Kumar! Chandran mentioned you were visiting. How are you?' Thirumalai, the septuagenarian owner of periya veedu, called out to him. Kumar stopped his cycle and walked over.

'I am doing well. How are you, ayya?'

'We survive. This is not America but we manage,' the old man replied, smiling.

'I am sure you more than just manage! How is Ramesh?'

'He's doing fine. But thambi, please find him a job in America. I hear they pay very well there. Is that so?' Thirumalai inquired.

'You also have huge expenses,' Kumar gave his well-practised reply. 'And why does Ramesh need a job? He is doing well, isn't he?'

'He could do better. Please see if you can take him to America. Initial expenses are not a problem.'

'Sure, I'll see what I can do,' said Kumar and took his leave.

Back on the road, Kumar could not resist thinking of the numerous times Thirumalai had struck him with whatever he could get his hands on for attempting to climb the bullock cart. The old man was now asking him to find his grandson a job. The times have definitely changed. He felt optimistic about the meeting with Kanaka aachi as he pedalled past what was left of Sengeerai forest into Rayavaram town.

Kanaka aachi's house was at the north end of town where the wealthy resided. A merry, middle-aged divorcee with a thriving business as a real estate agent, aachi lived in an old-fashioned, dilapidated Chettiar mansion that stretched from one block to another. The rest of her family lived in cities or were abroad and came to town for the occasional wedding or funeral. Aachi lived in a small portion of the house and did what she could for the upkeep of the rest of it. When Kumar arrived at the main gate, Kanaka aachi was in the courtyard busy supervising a handful of men cleaning the yard.

'Kumar, come in. I was just about to call you,' she said to him.

Kumar opened the gate and wheeled his bicycle inside. He parked it and sat down in the thinnai.

'Don't sit in the thinnai, come inside.'

'Post-Pongal cleaning, aachi?' inquired Kumar. It had been two weeks since the Pongal festival.

'We clean this place when I can afford it and when these men deign to come to my house! Come on inside, let me show you my new computer, you must tell me how it compares to your American ones.'

'You bought a new computer?'

'How else will I manage my business in the era of technology? All of Vikraman's friends and prospective clients send inquiries through email,' she explained as she walked inside.

'You have become high-tech, aachi!' Kumar said and tentatively followed her inside. He was conscious that this was the first time he was stepping inside a Chettiar mansion. He took in the series of courtyards, the ornate teak pillars around them and the shiny polished floors which were Italian marble or custom-made Aathangudi tiles. There were numerous rooms leading from the courtyard, and Kanaka aachi went inside one of them.

'This is my study,' she told Kumar as he entered through

the doorway. 'It was the accountant's room in my father's time and I used to be banished from it.'

Kumar did not answer as he was taking his time looking around. Aachi laughed at his expression of wonder.

'Kumar, stop looking at this old decrepit house as if it's the eighth wonder of the world!'

'But I've only seen these kinds of houses in films. It's a beautiful house; it's not really a house, it looks like a palace! You have to keep this pristine,' Kumar told her earnestly.

'Thank you, Kumar!' Aachi was glad that someone appreciated the house and the effort she put into it. 'My choices are to run a resort for foreigners or to rent it out for TV serial shoots. I don't mind the latter if they give me a part,' she said.

'Yes, you could be the evil mother-in-law bent on torturing your daughter-in-law!'

Aachi sighed. 'What do I know about sons and daughters-in-law? Now, sit down and tell me about your proposal. I am all ears. In fact, I have found the perfect house for you.'

'In the village?' Kumar sounded excited.

'Of course not. Why would anyone want to buy in the village? I found you the perfect house close to the Sivan temple street here in town. It is an old Chettiar outhouse with a few cents of land around it. The price is very attractive and the size is perfect for your family. If you like, we can see it right now. I have the keys.'

Kumar laughed uneasily and sat down. This is going to be difficult, he thought.

'All our relatives are in the village. My mother will not live in town. It makes sense to build in the village.'

'But people don't even want to live in town any more; they are moving to the cities.' When he said he wanted land to build a house, aachi hadn't expected Kumar to want to buy in Ayyanarpatti.

'I am quite sure about this, aachi,' Kumar said.

'Well, if you are determined to spend your money in the village, I can't stop you. Tell me where exactly you are looking to buy and I'll see what we have there.'

Kumar hesitated. Aachi would understand, that's why he had approached her instead of the other real estate brokers. 'Upper Street,' he said slowly.

Aachi stared at him, astonished. He surely couldn't be serious and she said so. 'You aren't serious, surely.'

'I am. What is the asking price in Upper Street?'

Aachi walked slowly towards the window and looked outside.

'I don't think your mother will be happy moving to Upper Street,' she said, finally.

'She'll be proud that her son can afford to buy her a house on Upper Street.'

'Will she really? Will she be happy if you uproot her from her own little world?'

'She'll still be in her village, nothing will be different.'

Aachi shook her head and turned around to face him.

'I think she will be much happier if you buy in town. She can visit everyone in the village whenever she wants to but she'll have all the conveniences of urban life.'

Kumar was getting impatient as they were going around in circles. 'Aachi, I am determined to buy in Upper Street in my own village. You tell me the market price and I'll pay it.'

Aachi looked at him thoughtfully. She had always liked Kumar – she remembered him as a boy when he used to walk past her house to go to school. He was quiet and studious and no trouble at all, her cousin who had taught him in high school used to say. Remarkable for someone from his background, she had heard. From all accounts, he had grown up to be a fine young man and was taking care of his family well. But he did not seem to understand what he was asking for now. It was not only difficult but it wasn't desirable to anyone except him. He was pursuing some misguided childhood dream without any understanding of the consequences. But the boy had come to her. She measured her words.

'Very well then,' she said finally. 'Chandran is selling the land behind his house. It's five cents.'

'What is the price?'

'It may be unaffordable for you but we can try. I can say it's for someone else. We have to be careful but it can be done if that's what you want,' aachi said.

'But…you mean to say he won't sell it if he knows I am the buyer?' Kumar protested.

'I don't see how he would.'

'He knows me well.'

'Then why don't you ask him directly? You can save my commission. I am out of the picture.' It was aachi's turn to be impatient. Kumar was just acting stupid.

'Aachi, don't play games with me,' Kumar said, frustrated. 'You know perfectly well why I can't. Because nobody, nobody from my family…or caste, no Dalit, has ever owned land in Upper Street.'

'Or anywhere else in the village. Your house is outside the village limits.'

Aachi did not want to say it so bluntly but he hadn't left her with a choice. Kumar continued as if he hadn't heard her.

'But this is the twenty-first century and I can buy land wherever I can afford to buy. I am ready to pay the asking price. What's the problem?'

'You are expecting your little village to move at your pace and that doesn't fit in with reality.'

Kumar had had enough. He had a lot of respect for aachi from his childhood days as she always stopped to talk to him and enquire about his studies. But this wasn't going anywhere.

'I came to buy land. There's no reason why you should behave like a feudal landlord and give me a lecture on caste relations.'

'Is it because I am a feudal landlord that you are sitting in my study? How many houses on Upper Street have you seen the inside of, boy?'

'You are so broadminded that you let a Dalit boy come into your study! What should I do now? Build a temple for you?' Kumar said angrily and stood up.

Ah, the boy has a temper, aachi thought, but it's not going to help.

'A temple for me! Not in your village, I hope. Who will let she who is separated from her husband into the inner sanctum? Oh, it's not just me, is it?' Aachi retorted knowing fully well that her remark would hit the mark.

It did, and Kumar turned pale. 'No one would stop Dalits if we wanted to enter the sanctum in Ayyanarpatti.'

'One of your neighbours tried it a few months ago. The priest had to perform rituals for three straight days to cleanse the premises, from what I heard,' aachi replied.

'Tall stories! I do not believe that in this day and age I cannot buy a house on Upper Street.'

Aachi shrugged. Kumar continued, 'You know what? I am going to speak to Chandran annan right now. I don't need your help on this.' Kumar left the study abruptly without looking back.

'Good luck,' Aachi called after him, and she meant it.

~

It was after dusk when Kumar turned his bicycle into Upper Street. He stopped in front of Chandran annan's house. He'd had enough time to think about what Kanaka aachi had said on his way home. She was still stuck in the last century despite appearances, he should not take her too seriously. He was quite the conformist himself, but a house on Upper Street had always been a dream. He had to ask Chandran annan. He wasn't an activist; he wasn't trying to prove a point. In his mind, it was very simple. In two weeks, he would be back in St Paul well removed from Ayyanarpatti and its many issues. But a house on Upper Street used to be an unachievable dream, and now, he was within striking distance. Money was not an issue.

'Kumar, there you are! Come inside. I was telling Raja that he should study like you and find work in America.' Chandran sounded welcoming, and Kumar's spirits soared. This is a positive sign, he thought. Kanaka aachi was overreacting.

He sat down in the thinnai. 'You don't need to worry about Raja. From what I remember, he did well in school,' he said.

'Uma,' Chandran called out to his daughter. 'Bring us some buttermilk.'

'I am quite full,' Kumar said, rubbing his stomach.

'So what? Buttermilk is good for the heat. You are not even used to the heat any more. You need to drink a lot of buttermilk; otherwise you will be dehydrated. Raja, come here. You can ask Kumar anna your questions.'

Raja, a shy boy in his late teens, stepped forward. Kumar remembered him from his school days; he was quite a few years behind Kumar.

'Isn't this your last year at school?'

'Yes, I'm not sure which college to choose next year.'

'What do you have in mind?' Kumar enquired.

'Manickam College nearby is good and I'll get in there. My friends say KAT in Coimbatore is better. But it's far away.'

'Far away?' Kumar laughed. 'Rubbish. Of course you have to take KAT if you get through.'

'Is that so?' Chandran jumped in. 'Is that really a good college, Kumar?'

'Yes, you should let Raja study there. The local Manickam College is not good at all – no proper facilities and it is run by rowdies.' Kumar knew what he was talking about.

'But in Coimbatore, we have to spend money on the hostel, don't we? It's also a big city, so the expenses will be rather high.' Chandran seemed unconvinced.

'You can always get educational loans. Anyway, once Raja gets a job after graduation, it won't matter.'

'That's true,' said Chandran. 'I'll think about it, Kumar. It's good you are here to give us some guidance.'

Kumar beamed. They were taking his advice seriously. Now was the time to broach the subject. He started to mumble something when Uma came out with a tray. Kumar and Uma used to be in the same class for a number of years but they had barely exchanged half a dozen words. Kumar knew she was engaged to be married in a few months. He looked up and smiled at her and she smiled back. She held the tray out to him. He took a tumbler in his hands and was about to drink from it when he noticed what he was holding. His hands shook. He put the aluminium tumbler firmly down on the thinnai.

There were two stainless steel tumblers left on the tray. Chandran took one and Raja took the other.

'What's wrong?' enquired Chandran. 'Drink the buttermilk.'

Kumar kept staring at the aluminium tumbler. He got up from the floor slowly. Chandran looked at him, puzzled.

'I have to hurry. I told amma I'd be back soon,' Kumar muttered. He picked up his bicycle that was leaning against the wall. He could not bring himself to ride it. He rolled it slowly all the way home.

Kanaka aachi was right. Nothing had changed. He would not have gotten past the thinnai unless there was some heavy lifting to be done in the house. So what if he was a software engineer in America making ten times the money anyone makes in his village? He would always be a pariah boy, which meant that he would be served in aluminium tumblers, and not be allowed access to the goddess. No stainless steel for him – they were meant only for upper caste people. Everyone had a place in the Ayyanarpatti hierarchy. He should not have forgotten his.

Kumar laughed bitterly. He was a fool to think his village would have changed with the times and become caste agnostic. By the time he reached home, he had made the decision. He would talk to his mother and convince her. The next morning, he would call Kanaka aachi and, if possible, see the house in town. A small Chettiar outhouse was sounding rather attractive. In fact, he was certain his mother and sister were going to be thrilled.

A New Release

'One day, you'll wake up and find me gone. The old hag would have finished me off. Close. The End,' Paapa whispered to Kalai, plunging a hypothetical kitchen knife in slow motion on to her heaving chest.

'Smile all you want! But you'll see the truth when I'm no more. At night, I sit up and wonder how she'll do it. I don't think it'll be a gas cylinder accident, that's very old-fashioned and she'd be booked under a dowry case. Is she planning to push me down the well? No, someone may see her. So what is she planning to do? She'll poison me. That herbalist quack came to the house a few days ago to give her a concoction, supposedly for her knees, but I know what it is – a slow-acting poison! She's already poisoning me!'

'Nobody is poisoning you. You are fine,' Kalai reassured her friend.

Paapa's insistence that her mother-in-law was going to murder her someday in the near future wasn't new. Only the mechanics of the imminent murder differed each week, depending on what was in vogue in the latest episodes of the popular television serials.

'I know it's difficult. But you are not making it any easier by pretending not to hear her,' she continued as she could clearly hear Paapa's mother-in-law calling for her from inside the house.

'What do you know about my life?' Paapa snapped. 'Your mother-in-law treats you like twenty-four-carat gold.'

'Gold indeed!'

'I wish I'd married into your family. Pandi would have done nicely. Instead I'm stuck in this wretched house!' Paapa struck her palm across her forehead and bemoaned her luckless fate.

'Pandi wouldn't have married you.' It came out before Kalai could stop herself.

'Why, is he holding out for someone like you?'

'Listen,' Kalai changed the subject. She knew there was no malice intended in her friend's question but she wasn't going to continue this discussion. 'We can go to the new Vijay movie next week. It's releasing on Friday and I'll get tickets. Are you up for it?'

'Of course I am up for it. But you think that bitch will let me go?' Paapa looked over her shoulder to make sure that her mother-in-law was out of hearing.

'It's a Vijay film, we have to go. Say you are accompanying me to the doctor. Now hurry, she's coming out to look for you.' Kalai did not want her to get into any more trouble. Paapa swiftly walked away from the hedge towards the water well. The old pulley creaked and the steel pail made its way down just as Paapa's mother-in-law opened the rear door and came into view.

Kalai walked back towards her kitchen. It was an

unusually cool morning, and there were a few dew drops still clinging to the leaves. She plucked a few jasmine flowers from the creeper and inhaled their fragrance. She wound a couple of them between her well-oiled plaits and started humming a tune from the soundtrack of an old Vijay movie, savouring her last few moments of peace before her two-year-old woke up.

'Is Paapa complaining about her mother-in-law again?'

Kalai looked up, surprised. She hadn't expected her mother-in-law to be back from the farm so early.

'Yes, athai. She has nothing else to do.' Kalai agreed with Pachaiamma on almost everything, a partial explanation for why they got along so well, relative to the neighbours in any case. Pachaiamma started telling her the story of Paapa's wedding for the umpteenth time, and how she had advised her friend Valli next door not to pursue the alliance. But Valli was too greedy: Paapa was bringing in five hundred grams of gold and that was all that mattered. Look at Valli now, unhappy, always quarrelling with Paapa who, just as Pachaiamma had predicted, wasn't suitable for the family.

'Aravind's fever has not subsided.' Kalai swerved her away from her favourite topic with practised ease. For all the melodrama, Paapa was a sweet girl and a real friend to Kalai. She couldn't let Pachaiamma continue with the character assassination.

'Yes, I heard him a few times during the night…Is that him crying?'

Both women rushed inside the house to tend to the boy. But they didn't get very far as Pandi was already carrying a bawling Aravind down the staircase.

'Can't you hear the poor child coughing and crying? Is this the time for you women to catch up on village gossip?' Pandi asked as he handed Aravind to Kalai.

'I have to cook in the morning and athai has to tend to the farm. You could wake up early and take care of him,' Kalai shot back. She rocked the baby back and forth, and he calmed down.

'Ah, will you go to work then?'

Pachaiamma knew if she did not intervene they would bicker the whole day. Kalai never had a disagreement with her, but she made up for that by picking on her son every single day. In the beginning, she had admonished them both and asked them to behave like adults but it didn't help and she had come to accept it over time. On good days, she reluctantly admitted to herself that their non-stop back and forth enlivened her otherwise dull day and brought a smile to her lips.

'The idlis are on the table. Sit down,' she said to Pandi and turned towards Kalai. 'And you, give Aravind that syrup the doctor prescribed.'

Pandi sat down at the dining table. His mother served him three idlis and poured hot sambar on top, the way he liked it.

'Aravind has to be taken to the clinic,' she told him as he gobbled down the idlis.

'I don't have the time right now but I can take him later in the day. Around eleven.' He looked askance at Kalai but addressed his mother. 'Ask her to be ready on the dot. I don't have much time to waste.'

'When was I late?'

'Last week, for the registrar office,' Pandi replied promptly.

'I wasn't late. Aravind refused to get ready.'

'How come he never refuses to get ready when you go to the cinema?'

'That's enough! I don't understand how you manage to live under the same roof,' Pachaiamma intervened once more. 'Here, have one more idli. And tell me what I should tell Ganesan regarding the wedding.'

Pandi stopped eating. He suddenly seemed to have lost his appetite. He looked down at the plate and did not answer.

'Well?' Pachaiamma persisted.

'I haven't thought about it,' he said finally.

'What is there to think about?' She was not going to let it go easily.

'I am late for work.' Pandi got up from the table. He went to the washbasin and washed his hands before running upstairs, two steps at a time.

Pachaiamma sighed. She looked at Kalai. 'Has he told you anything?'

Kalai shook her head.

'Why don't you talk to him? He will listen.'

Kalai laughed. 'He won't listen to me. Why would he?'

Pandi came back down, this time with his office folders. He walked to the television stand and picked up the keys to his motorbike. As if on cue, Aravind started crying.

'I was hoping he wouldn't make a fuss. Aravind, I promise to come back later and take you on the bike.' He jingled the keys in front of the boy, who cried louder.

'I'll take him upstairs. Don't start the bike here please

– roll it until you get to the junction. If he hears it, he will never stop.'

Kalai carried her son up the stairs and into the bedroom. She put him down on the floor, went to the Godrej almirah and pulled out a large model of Thomas the Tank Engine.

'Look here, your favourite train. Appa got this from Singapore for you,' she told her son but Aravind wasn't interested in the engine. He walked out of the room and towards the stairs. Kalai ran after him.

'The poor child is ill, why can't you take care of him?' Pachaiamma shouted from downstairs.

'He doesn't stop crying, he won't listen to me.' Kalai was losing her patience. The boy cried all the time. What was she supposed to do?

Pachaiamma came up to the room and lifted the boy. He stopped crying immediately. 'Poor baby, come with me. We don't want to stay with people who make us cry.' She disappeared downstairs with her grandson.

Kalai went inside her room and closed the door. She had not slept well the previous night due to Aravind's fever. Perhaps she could catch up on sleep before Pandi came home to fetch them. She did not mind not seeing her son for a while; in fact, she didn't want to see him for a while. Let her athai take care of him. She sat down on the bed. Why hadn't anyone told her it was exhausting to take care of a child? She had been the youngest in her family, and never had to take care of her siblings. When she was younger, she had wished that she had been the firstborn, as she could lord over her brothers and sisters. But now she knew better. The thought of her siblings made her wistful. She missed them and her native village. Everything was different here in Ayyanarpatti, even the farmlands. Back home, the soil was much more fertile. It was as if the crops themselves liked to grow there. She preferred the Perumal temple in her village to the Kamakshi temple here – sure, the Perumal temple was smaller and less ornate, but He was more powerful in her opinion. She had prayed to Perumal for a mother-in-law who treated her well and a caring husband who bought her everything she wanted. Perumal had listened and delivered.

~

Kalai had to be woken up when Pandi arrived at eleven. He wasn't happy to be kept waiting, but was glad to be vindicated and he smirked at Kalai when she finally came down. At the clinic, the doctor gave Aravind a shot, and prescribed a load of antibiotics. Pandi picked up the medicines from the clinic's pharmacy, and walked towards his bike where Kalai and Aravind were waiting. Aravind was perched on the driver's seat, turning the handle and pretending to steer.

'Pandi, since we are here anyway…' Kalai began with a wide smile. This was her chance.

'No,' snapped Pandi, before Kalai could complete her sentence. 'I have to be back at work.'

'But it'll only take five minutes,' she pleaded.

'You can reserve your cinema ticket yourself and take the bus home.' He was going to be late for the accounts inspection at work, and was in no mood to indulge her. Also, he was sick of her obsession with Vijay and didn't understand what she saw in these films. Vijay saving the world. Vijay protecting the honour of women everywhere. As if the rest of them had been castrated! He wasn't going to buy her tickets and that was that.

'But Aravind is ill. How will I carry him on the bus? We won't get tickets if we don't reserve them today and this movie is going to be a super hit.' Kalai couldn't bear the thought of her friends seeing the new Vijay movie before her. She had to try harder.

'You can take the bus home.' Pandi did not budge.

Kalai sighed. Time to play the trump card. 'If only your brother was here…' she trailed off.

He should have seen it coming. 'Selva doesn't like cinema,' he answered.

'But he would have bought tickets for me.'

'When you speak to him this Sunday, tell him to fly back from Singapore for the day and buy you tickets.'

Kalai turned away, a lone tear making its way slowly down her cheek. Aravind continued to play with the bike handle. Pandi hesitated. He was not going to give in yet again. He was thinking of something appropriate to say when they were accosted by a loud voice.

'Pandi! How are you?'

Pandi looked up to see Chandran walking towards them. Chandran was a portly man of about fifty, the village busybody, an opportunistic sidekick of Councillor Muthu. Pandi had not seen Chandran for a while, but he had heard that Chandran had recently been rather active in politics.

'Chandran anna. How are you?'

'I am doing very well, thanks to Lord Pillayar. I was with Muthu in Chennai the past couple of weeks.'

'But when did you become a party member?'

'When I realized that our nation needs people like me to work for the well-being of her people. And who is this here? How are you, Kalai?' He smiled at her and pinched Aravind's cheeks. Aravind rushed into his mother's arms.

'I am fine, mama,' replied Kalai, in a measured tone. She had lived in Ayyanarpatti long enough to know that Chandran had to be dealt with carefully.

'But why are you looking so sad? Did this fellow say anything?' Chandran looked suspiciously from Kalai to Pandi and back.

'No, mama. Aravind is ill and I'm worried,' Kalai said quickly. The last thing she wanted to do was give Chandran fodder for gossip.

'Did the doctor give him an injection?' he enquired.

'Yes. He has also prescribed medicines.'

'Our medicines don't work, they are all counterfeit,' Chandran said authoritatively. 'You ask Selva to send those foreign medicines from Singapore – they are much more effective.'

'I'll tell him when he calls,' Kalai said, smiling.

'Good. How is Selva doing?'

'He's fine. He has applied for permanent residence,' Pandi answered.

'PR is very good if he gets it. Then he can do something on his own there instead of working for someone else. He can take you as well, can't he?' Chandran turned to ask Kalai.

'What will I do there, mama? I am happy here.'

Kalai realized her mistake as soon as the words came

out of her mouth. This was the opening Chandran was waiting for.

Chandran smiled and said in a sweet voice. 'Are you saying that your brother-in-law keeps you so happy that you don't need your husband?'

Kalai returned his sugary sweet smile. 'My athai keeps me so happy that I don't feel the need to go anywhere. Somebody has to be here to take care of her.' She was very much capable of playing the part of the dutiful daughter-in-law.

Pandi had had enough by now. 'Chandran anna, we have to go. I'm already late for work.'

'I don't know what's wrong with you young men of today. Never want to talk to us old people,' Chandran protested.

Pandi ignored him and started the bike.

~

Aravind slept well into the afternoon as a result of the antibiotics. His temperature had steadily come down since the morning. Kalai spent the time listlessly changing channels on the TV – the afternoon serials were over, and it would be a few hours before the evening mega serials began. She considered going over to Paapa's, but didn't feel up to hearing her friend's newest murder paranoia. She also had to think of a way of getting tickets for next week's release, now that Pandi had refused. Paapa was useless in getting her husband to procure tickets; she would have to go to town by herself, Kalai decided.

Pachaiamma was sprawled on the veranda, waking up leisurely from her usual afternoon nap. The late afternoon breeze was soothing, tempting her to lie down for a while longer. She could see the sky from where she lay; rain clouds were gathering – it looked like they would get Maasi showers this year. Her reverie was broken by the sound of a motorcycle. She hurriedly got up.

'Ganesa anna, come in,' she welcomed Ganesan, who parked his motorcycle under the tree in front of the house.

'Good news, Pachai! I have a new horoscope which is a perfect fit, so I came immediately to see you.' Ganesan sounded excited.

'Please sit down, anna.' She turned towards the living room and called in a loud voice. 'Kalai, Ganesan mama is here. Can you bring some tea?'

Ganesan sat down on the floor next to Pachaiamma and pulled out the girl's photo and horoscope from his yellow cloth bag. He was the official marriage broker for Ayyanarpatti. He worked with his counterparts in the neighbouring villages to arrange appropriate alliances. He had an encyclopedic knowledge of all eligible young men and women of marriageable age in the entire district, categorized by class, caste, education and geography. He had started looking for a bride for Pandi a few months back at Pachaiamma's behest but nothing very promising had appeared until now.

The prospective bride hailed from the village of Sirungudi, a few kilometres from Ayyanarpatti. Her two brothers had government jobs in town and were well settled, in Ganesan's view. Pachaiamma was pleased as she believed that a girl should have brothers. They would always be a source of support for the family. In addition, this girl was educated to the degree level and she worked as a teacher in a primary school. She could easily get a transfer to a nearby village, Ganesan informed her.

'Oh!' Pachaiamma did not seem as happy as he had expected her to be. 'But will a working girl be suitable for our family?'

'Of course! Who wants to say no to one more salary? Don't be stuck in the dark ages, Pachai!'

'But I'm getting old and not able to do so many things like I used to. Who will look after the house?' Pachaiamma wasn't entirely convinced.

'You already have one daughter-in-law in the house. Kalai can manage easily.'

'Kalai is finding it difficult with Aravind around. How will the poor girl manage?'

'Pachai, have I ever been wrong? Don't worry about these minor things. You can be sure that between Kalai and this girl, they will work it out…Kalai!' He looked up as Kalai came in with the tea. He took the tumbler from her and took a sip.

'I was telling your athai that you will definitely be able to manage the household if Pandi were to marry a working girl.'

'What does she do?' Kalai enquired politely.

'She is a teacher at the primary school.'

'Is this her photo?'

'Yes, what do you think?' Ganesan handed the photo to Kalai.

'She is dark. Like the night,' she said immediately. Ganesan was taken aback but not entirely surprised.

'Like you are Aishwarya Rai,' Pachaiamma retorted.

'But your son is fair. How can he marry this dark girl?'

'Why don't we ask him?' Ganesan said.

'We cannot ask him anything. Any talk of marriage and he runs forty-two miles!'

'Why is that, I wonder?' Ganesan was puzzled. 'If he waits too long, all the good alliances will disappear.'

'But how are we going to convince him?' asked Pachaiamma.

'Kalai, can't you speak to your brother-in-law? He will listen to you.'

'He does not listen to anyone.'

'Everyone knows he dances to your...' Ganesan caught himself. 'I mean, he listens to you.'

'But how can I ask him to marry a dark girl?'

'Last time you said the girl was cross-eyed. The one before that didn't have any education. Do you think some Ramba Urvashi is going to come down from the skies and marry your brother-in-law?' Ganesan was getting impatient.

'But you are only bringing ratchasis, mama!'

'Kalai, that's enough,' her mother-in-law interrupted. 'Aravind has woken up – I can hear him.'

Kalai reluctantly went inside the house.

Ganesan sipped his tea. 'How is Selva?' he asked after a while.

'He rang on Sunday. If Pandi were to get married, he'll come for the wedding.'

'If all goes well, we can have the wedding in a couple of months.'

'That is what I am praying for,' Pachaiamma sighed.

'Selva has not visited us in two and a half years. He has not even seen Aravind yet.'

'Poor Kalai, it would do her good.'

'Yes. She saw him for two weeks after their wedding but hasn't seen him ever since. And it's time I had a granddaughter.'

'True, true. Can you talk to Pandi? Between you and Kalai I am sure he will agree to it.'

'I'll talk to him. I am not sure if she will. Women don't like other women in the house.'

'Especially when there are not enough men to go around.'

'Anna!'

'Pachai, you know I did not mean anything.' He put his tea tumbler down and got up. 'I will be back in a couple of days. You ask Pandi to think about this girl.'

~

'Kalai…'

Pandi paused in front of the door to the room. Kalai looked at the clock. She had been expecting him.

'Come in but be quiet,' she whispered. 'He just fell asleep.'

Pandi stepped inside. 'How is he doing?' he asked.

'He is recovering.'

'Good. I came to give you this,' he said, and handed her an office envelope.

'What's this?' she asked him, though she knew perfectly well what it contained.

'Tickets for next week. We can go for the first show on Friday.'

'But you don't like Vijay.'

'If Selva was here, he would have done the same.' He felt the need to explain.

Kalai took the envelope from him and put it on the bedside table. 'Yes, he would have.'

Pandi looked intently at the sleeping boy for a few minutes. Kalai looked at the jackfruit tree outside the window. After a while, Pandi cleared his throat.

'What did Ganesan mama say?'

'Didn't your mother tell you?'

'She did, but you also saw the photo.'

'The girl is dark.'

'Hmm.'

'Did your mother not show you the photo?'

'No. She said the girl is a teacher. She can teach Aravind too.'

Kalai looked up at him. 'But you said you did not want to get married.'

Pandi shifted uncomfortably. He knew he was entering uncharted waters, but he wanted to know where things stood. He was not entirely disinclined to the idea of being married. It was the right age, most of his friends were married already. But, but he also liked Kalai a lot. One might say a little more than the typical brother-in-law should.

'How long can I remain single?'

'Your brother had the burden of family, so he had to work hard and ensure you had a job before he got married. With you, it's different. You are settled.'

'You are making me feel guilty.'

'The dark teacher will come to this house and you will

take her to Vijay movies. You won't tell her that you don't like Vijay.' Kalai couldn't help it.

'Kalai!'

'Ssh. He is sleeping.' She rubbed the boy's hair. 'His father will be here for the wedding. Aravind misses him.'

'He doesn't know him.'

'He talks over the phone.'

'Yes.' He hesitated. 'You think I don't take care of Aravind?'

'You do,' she paused. 'Now.'

'Nothing will change.'

Kalai shrugged.

'I am going to ask amma to proceed unless you think…'

'It has nothing to do with me.'

Pandi shook his head and walked to the door. He stepped out and closed the door behind him. Kalai sat down on the bed and looked at her sleeping son.

'PR,' she whispered to him. 'Your father, the real one, needs to get PR in Singapore, and take us away from here. Do you hear me? That is what you need to tell your father when he calls on Sunday.'

Her eyes fell on the envelope with the movie tickets lying next to the sleeping boy. She stared at them for a long time. Pandi would be lost to her soon, but until she can be with her husband, she will at least have Vijay. She fell asleep next to her son dreaming of the new movie.

Scenes from a Scandal

1 Aachi Spots an Opportunity

Terraced mansions that stretch from one street to the next.

Wide courtyards with carved pillars made of Burma teak.

Belgian mirrors in the bedrooms, Italian marble on the verandahs, handmade Aathangudi flooring inside the house.

Garages that are often mistaken for old stables.

A Chettinad mansion may well be the ultimate lap of luxury, but then there are a few things that the marketing brochures forget to mention, Kanaka aachi thought to herself, as she read the description of an old friend's house in a nearby town, now converted to a home-stay. They always forget to mention that the courtyards in these houses often open into tiny, windowless rooms. Bathrooms are invariably outside the house in the far end of the backyard. The staircases are high and narrow, and the steps are far apart from each other, making it an impossible climb for anyone past the age of fifty. A Chettinad house is indeed paradise, but only for someone who doesn't have to live in it for a lifetime.

Aachi surveyed her dominion from her office, a room that she had managed, with great difficulty, to convert into a functional space to meet her requirements – natural light, fresh air, a desk with a computer and a couple of chairs. This mansion has been her home for more than half a century now. She had left the house for a short two years many decades ago to start a new and exciting life in the Land of the Free, but that had ended in tragedy. She returned home, grown up and jaded, the first divorcee in Rayavaram town.

Her father, overly fond of his daughter as the tongues wagged, left the mansion to her in his will. Vikraman took it well, all considered. After all, what did he need this house for other than the occasional wedding? Having his sister here meant that it would be well-maintained, unlike the other houses in town, and he could bring his family to experience the rustic life in relative comfort once every couple of years. For her part, Kanaka aachi wished she hadn't inherited this house. A simple one-bedroom house with a small garden would have served her much better, but this mansion was hers now, and she was duty-bound to live in it, and spend most of her hard-earned money towards its upkeep. Her next project was a bedroom in the ground floor; she wouldn't be able to climb up those stairs much longer. The cash would materialize this year if her luck held. Real estate had slowed down in the past several months but it hadn't hit her hard yet. Her thoughts turned to work.

There was significant interest in the land close to the town bus stand, adjacent to where the Moorthy brothers were building their shopping complex, the first of its kind in Rayavaram. The price of the land had gone up threefold in the past year. Aachi knew the landowner – the retired schoolmaster from Ayyanarpatti. Just yesterday, she had been to the village for his daughter's wedding. He would get a good price for it, and he could probably do with the cash. If not, she could always interest him in reinvesting elsewhere. She unlocked her phone and dialled.

2 After the Wedding

In Ayyanarpatti, Siva master sat in his thinnai contemplating the aftermath of the wedding, almost certainly the last that this house would host. The bride and groom had left for Chennai once all the ceremonies and formalities were completed. But the house was still strewn with flowers and turmeric-coated rice grains used to bless the newly-weds. The cleaning crew would arrive any moment now. A teenage boy was busy untying the tube lights from the light poles. The bright red shamiana would remain in place for another couple of days along with the plantain that adorned the wooden poles holding up the canopy. The chef's helpers had left, but the chef was still in Ayyanarpatti, drinking with the young ones in the mango grove. His dues had yet to be paid.

'Neru, come in. You look like a bus conductor with that bag under your arm!' Siva master teased his friend and invited him inside.

'Just like the poor bus conductor, none of this money is mine!'

Neru handed the large leather bag to Siva and sat down next to him. He opened his long register that held the accounts for the wedding.

'You count the cash, I'll do the totals and let us see if the account tallies. I was writing down names and gifts non-stop for nearly three hours yesterday. I reckon you have a decent collection here.'

Neru was referring to the wedding gifts, in the form of money or gold, that guests had brought the day before. A lawyer by profession, Neru had the unofficial charge of collection and accounting for all weddings in Ayyanarpatti.

'What you give, you get back,' Siva replied, philosophically.

He opened the bag and took out the first set of currency notes. He wet his index finger with his tongue and started counting. Neru read out names and numbers aloud as he went through his register: 'Chandran – 501, Muthu – 1001, Selva – 301, a measure of rice, Mari – a gold ring...didn't specify the weight.'

'I gave a ring of 4 grams for his daughter's wedding last year, he'd have done the same,' Siva said and continued counting.

An hour later, their accounting was complete, and there were neat piles of cash set aside for catering, lighting, furniture, cleaning, and miscellaneous. Siva placed the gold jewellery in a separate bag.

'The gold goes to Chithra. I'll give it to her when she comes home for Deepavali,' he said.

'Why wait so long? I hope you are going to see her before that.'

'I don't think so. There is enough for me to do here. The kids come home for classes every day and there are a few other things I need to take care of.'

Neru felt sorry for the schoolmaster. His wife had died

when his only daughter was five. His parents had taken care of Chithra but they passed away a few years ago. Now that Chithra had left for her in-laws' house, Siva master would be totally alone in this large house. Despite his bravado, Neru knew that the master was going to be very lonely.

Siva continued, oblivious to his friend's thoughts. 'I'm thinking of farming some of the land that has been lying barren for years now.'

'There is a reason they are barren, Master. Good luck with finding farm labour!'

Before Siva could reply, his phone rang.

'Kanaka aachi!' He sounded surprised.

3 A Daughter Is Troubled

Chithra was settling down well in Chennai. Her husband was kind and gentle, and had agreed to let her take up a job at a private college close to home. Her in-laws were like in-laws everywhere, and she worked around them as best as she could. She thought of her father less frequently than she had thought she would, which made her feel all the more guilty. She made it a point to call him twice a day, and became worked up if he didn't answer, which seemed to occur surprisingly often. He was busy with tuitions, or running errands in town, or he was with Neru mama. Initially, Chithra thought her father was trying to hide his loneliness from her, but he sounded truly happy and content over the phone. She knew him well enough to know that he wasn't faking it. She was a tad disappointed that he seemed to be doing so well without her.

Then there was this strange talk the other day of selling the land next to the bus stand in Rayavaram. He said it would fetch a good price and he was going to reinvest the proceeds from the sale. It hadn't occurred to Chithra until then that her father could be in financial trouble, and she chastised herself for not having caught it earlier. He had spent extravagantly on her wedding and it was quite possible that he was in need of money. But when she tried to broach the subject with him and asked him whether she should speak to her husband, he had become indignant and defensive. She didn't push it. Her marriage was in its honeymoon period and she wanted to keep it that way as long as possible. But her father's atypical behaviour was making her uneasy, and she decided to have a chat with Neru mama to put her mind to rest.

4 Councillor Muthu Harbours a Nagging Suspicion

Councillor Muthu was in town to inspect the new shopping complex that was to be inaugurated in a few weeks. Thanks to him, a mid-level party functionary, an ex-MLA no less, had kindly agreed to grace the occasion and cut the ribbon on the auspicious day. Muthu visited the site once a week to ensure that the arrangements for the inauguration were going as per plan.

'The stage has to be moved here, this is better for the cameras. I'll make sure that the posters of the leader reach you within the week. They have to be plastered on all the walls…'

'But…'

'Do you think he inaugurates minor shopping complexes? The only reason he agreed to do this was because I personally requested him on your behalf. If the arrangements aren't as per his specifications…'

'Don't worry, Muthu. Everything will be as you want it. Come back in a week and you'll see for yourself,' the owners reassured him.

Muthu gave them a few more directions and took his leave. He walked to his bike and was about to kick-start it when he noticed a familiar face behind the building site. Kanaka aachi, the town's only lady broker, seemed to be holding what looked like a skipping rope looped around her neck. A moment later, she raised it high and skipped! Muthu rubbed his eyes. She did it again but this time, she hopped. Next to her, a man who was a double of the venerable Siva master was clapping his hands and laughing like a five-year-old boy. Perplexed, he walked towards them. Kanaka aachi and Siva master noticed him, and looked at each other, visibly embarrassed.

'Hello Muthu,' Siva master called out to him. 'What brings you here?'

'Arrangements for the inauguration.' He pointed to the shopping complex. 'Former MLA is coming to cut the ribbon, and there is no one else to supervise everything,' he said. As he got closer, he got a good look at Kanaka aachi's skipping rope. It happened to be a measuring tape. She noticed him looking at it and blushed deeply.

'We are waiting for the surveyors to come and measure the plot,' she offered an explanation.

'They were supposed to be here half an hour ago. Always late,' Siva added.

Muthu looked at him in surprise. He had no idea that the modest schoolmaster owned land outside the village. 'Master, you own this land?'

Siva nodded. 'I bought it decades ago when Chithra's mother was alive. Kan…aachi has found a buyer and I am going to sell it,' he answered.

Muthu looked at aachi suspiciously before turning to Siva. 'How much are you selling it for?'

'Around a lakh per cent,' aachi answered for Siva.

Muthu was astonished. 'But master, you should get twice as much for this land.' He walked closer to Siva and lowered his voice. 'You can't trust this woman. Leave this to me,' he whispered.

Siva shook his head. 'Thanks, but I've already accepted the advance. I can't go back now,' he said.

Muthu looked from Siva to Kanaka aachi and back again. 'Sure, sure. I understand.'

5 Nithya Drops Off a Few Books

A few days later, on a toasty Pankuni evening, young Nithya stopped by the master's house to drop off a few library books he had asked for. Siva liked to read, and Nithya was always borrowing books for him from her college library. She had a soft corner for the schoolmaster; he had been instrumental in her managing to secure admission in a halfway decent college. Also, she felt it was her duty to provide him some well-needed company once in a while, especially since his daughter had left home.

As she parked her bicycle and went inside the house,

she was surprised to see that there were only a handful of children leaving his house at that time of day.

'Have you given them all a holiday, master?' she asked.

Every child of school-going age in Ayyanarpatti came to Siva in the evenings for tuitions. It didn't matter whether they went to the local government school (which hardly anyone did nowadays) or one of the many expensive private schools in town. The parents knew they would learn more from the schoolmaster.

'Well, some of them have stopped coming,' Siva said, unlike his usual self, his voice guarded.

'Why, is there a new master in our village?' Nithya was surprised. Nothing happened in this village without her being aware of it, or so she wanted it to be.

'I don't know of any new master. But does this mean you haven't been warned about coming to see me?'

'Why...oh...' A bulb seemed to go on inside Nithya, and she tapped her head hard. 'Now I know why everyone is so curious about these books I bring you from the library. I thought Ayyanarpatti had suddenly turned literary!'

'That would be the day,' Siva said, smiling.

'I wouldn't worry about all this, master. The kids will be back once their marks go down this year. You just wait.'

'Marks aren't as important as morals.'

Nithya shrugged. 'I wouldn't know much about either. Both terribly overrated, if you ask me. I need to be off, master.'

Siva watched her leave, thoughtfully. That girl was precocious and one never knew what to make of her. But he was glad that she didn't think ill of him and that gave him an inkling of hope. Perhaps Chithra would understand. Love has no age, after all.

6 Ayyanarpatti Has a Visitor

Councillor Muthu turned around at the sound of a car turning into Upper Street. Aachi's old Maruti 800 was weaving its way through the main street. Muthu recognized aachi's gaunt profile in the driver's seat but the car passed by too quickly for him to recognize anyone else. The car continued up the street but did not stop where he was expecting it to stop. It turned into one of the side lanes and disappeared from sight.

'Did you see who was in the car?' he asked Nithya, who was sitting on the steps of the house next door, a humungous book on engineering mechanics open on her lap.

'Ah, the councillor is blind!' she mocked him. 'Kumar's mother and sister.'

Muthu ignored the taunt for the moment. He needed more information from her.

'What are they doing with aachi?'

'How could the omniscient councillor not know?'

'Nithya, this is a serious matter. You have no idea how…'

'Oh, shut up. Kumar is buying a house in town. Since he is back in America, his family had to go to the registrar office for registration.'

Muthu's jaw dropped.

'That pariah boy is buying a house? Where?'

'An old Chettiar outhouse near the Sivan temple.'

'Why can't he buy in the village?'

'Were you offering him your land?'

'How did he…I'll talk to him when he comes back. But what has that woman got to do with Kumar buying…oh, I see, she's the broker?'

Nithya didn't bother to answer and Muthu continued.

'She seems to be doing quite well. Just from our village, she has so many clients – Kumar and now Siva master. The master is completely under her spell, did you know that?' Muthu asked her. Nithya pretended not to hear him.

The Maruti 800 came back up the street. This time, it stopped in front of the master's house.

'Look, look where she's going. Shameless! I am going to call some people and put a full stop to this once and for all.' He walked to the house across the street. 'Chandran anna!' he shouted.

'Full stop to what?' Nithya asked.

'You go inside. You shouldn't be watching this.' He waved her away. Nithya obediently got up and went inside. She continued to the far end of the narrow house and out into the backyard, ignoring her mother's calls. She deftly climbed up and down two fences before reaching Siva's backyard. She went up the steps and knocked on the back door.

Aachi left Siva's house a few minutes later. She started her car and drove slowly through the silent mob that had gathered on Upper Street.

7 Chithra Learns of Her Father's Transgressions

Chithra went shopping for the fourth time that day. 'I forgot to get detergent,' she told her in-laws and stepped out. She needed some time to think and to take calls from Paapa and Lalitha who were updating her with the latest. A very unlikely crisis was threatening to wreck her young life, and she had no idea whom to believe or what to do.

She didn't believe it at first when Lalitha got around to telling her about the village headlines of the past several days. The villagers were vile, she thought. Since she wasn't around, they were giving her poor father a hard time. Aachi was an acquaintance and a successful broker; he was meeting her to sell the land.

How much land does he own that he has to live with the broker?

That had hurt. Then, there was the story of how aachi had visited their house in the village intending to stay the night, and had to be forcibly sent back.

Shameful!

Aachi was richer than all of them put together; there was no reason for her to take a fancy to her father. It didn't make any sense.

Who knows what that wanton woman wants? We are the ones who have to be careful.

And then Neru mama had called her. He didn't mention aachi but insisted that Chithra invite her father to Chennai, and get him to stay there for a little while. The master's health wasn't what it used to be, he said, but Chithra knew better.

What would she tell her husband and in-laws, she asked her friends. She couldn't tell them that they had to take her father in so that she could keep an eye on him and make sure he didn't stray!

Lie. Tell them you miss him.
The kids have stopped going to him for tuitions. There is talk of more action.

She didn't have a choice any more. She had to get him out of Ayyanarpatti.

8 A Brother Is Concerned

'Kanaka...'

Vikraman was standing in his sister's office, pacing, looking outside on to the street. His coffee cup lay untouched on aachi's desk. He had come to Rayavaram a couple of days ago for a wedding, and was due to leave for Chennai in an hour. He was dreading this conversation, but he couldn't possibly leave without having spoken to her. There had been too many insinuations by too many people during the past two days that he just could not let it pass. He wasn't averse to his little sister having her own life but there was something called family honour that mattered, and there were some lines one didn't cross in a place like this.

'What is it?' aachi asked him, nonchalantly. She knew what was coming, but she wasn't going to make it any easier for him. He was the one who'd had the easy life.

'You have done a wonderful job with the house.'

'There is more to do. It is a money guzzler, this house.'

Vikraman nodded. 'But you have got to stop!' he blurted out.

'Stop living in this house?'

'No, your real estate business. You don't need it, we don't need it. I'll take care of everything.'

Aachi laughed uneasily. 'But that's not what you said before. You've always wanted me to be independent, be my own master. You've even sent clients my way.'

'You aren't getting any younger.'

'You are older than me and you run a conglomerate.'

'That's different.'

'How?'

Vikraman sat down in a chair. There was no point in beating about the bush. He and his sister were always direct with one another and despite their differences it had served them well over the years. This was no time to change it.

'Who is this schoolmaster?'

Aachi stared out of the window at nothing. What should she tell him? That she was in love? In all honesty, how much could she tell him without sounding like his adolescent daughter?

'Kanaka, people talk in this place,' Vikraman continued.

'People have always talked where I am concerned.'

'But you don't need to go through this unnecessary gossip any more. Tell you what, come stay with us until this thing blows over.'

'Until what blows over?'

'We have our family honour to think of.'

'Appa didn't think of family honour when I came back home battered. He wasn't ashamed of me.'

'It wasn't your fault then.'

'And now it is?'

'Does this man, this schoolmaster, does he live here with you as…as they say?'

'His house is in a nearby village. He lives there.'

'And there is nothing between you two?'

'I am selling his land for him.'

'That is all there is to it?'

'Vikraman, I am not your fifteen-year-old daughter.'

'Promise me you won't do anything silly.'

'Don't be ridiculous.'

Vikraman sighed in relief and smiled at her. He drank up the coffee in one shot and got up to leave. He would be fine, aachi concluded. He would get over it. Some day.

9 The Schoolmaster Says Goodbye

Chithra pleaded with her father to stay with them in Chennai for a few weeks. Siva finally made up his mind to leave; there was no point in letting the poor girl worry unnecessarily. He had to make up his mind either way. He visited Neru to hand him a few documents and the spare keys to his house. He wasn't planning to be back for a while, and wanted to make sure Neru had everything that may be required in his absence.

'I can take care of all this, not a problem. How long will you be gone?' Neru asked his friend.

'I am not sure yet.'

'Chithra'll be glad to have you there. I…I really think this is the best course of action given the situation here. The villagers are determined to keep away from you.'

'After all that I have done for their children!' Siva exclaimed bitterly.

'All that's forgotten when something like this happens. I must admit I never thought you would fall into this sort of a trap…situation, but you haven't been yourself since the wedding.'

'True, true. I have been a different person since the wedding.' He looked closely at Neru and continued, 'I feel… young.'

'We can't afford the luxury,' Neru said abruptly and Siva got up, as if on cue.

'No, we can't.'

10 The End

The last time anybody saw Kanaka aachi or Siva master, together or separately, was on the last day of the month, outside the taluk registrar office. Nithya, playing hookey from college, happened to be passing by when she saw them come out of the office, holding hands. Before she could cycle over, they got into aachi's car and drove away. An investigation by Councillor Muthu a few days later revealed a registered civil marriage.

A New Beginning

It is universally acknowledged that the first day of Chithirai is a new day, distinct from the day before and the day after, but opinion remains divided on whether it is the beginning of a new year, the Tamil New Year, in our case. A few years ago, the state's ruling party decreed the New Year of the Tamils begins on the first of Thai to coincide with Pongal as it had done in ancient times, instead of on the first of Chithirai, as it did in more recent times. The then opposition party, when they came back to power, promptly reverted the start of the year back to the first of Chithirai, the only beneficiaries of this back and forth calendar change being the outfits who print and sell banners announcing start of discount sales.

This debate, however, was irrelevant to Subbiah as, New Year or not, he had offered prayers and gratitude to the land that yielded his crops on the first day of Chithirai from as far back as he could remember, and he had every intention of continuing the practice until his dying day. He woke up earlier than usual, performed his ablutions, cut the plantain leaves and waited patiently for Rukkamma by the sugar cane field. He had spent the night on the string cot next to the farm shed. He had started sleeping there years ago when the old farmhand who guarded the farm at night died of snakebite. It was meant to be a temporary arrangement until they found a replacement watchman but they never did. Not that Subbiah had any complaints. He'd rather spend his nights by his crops than at home.

He looked up at the sky after a while, sighed and walked towards Upper Street. The sun wasn't going to wait for his wife to get there. At home, Lalitha, his daughter-in-law, gave him fresh rice, pongal and steamed dumplings in a tiffin carrier. Subbiah traced his way back, silently thanking his daughter-in-law for having remembered the offerings. Hardly anyone in the village performed the land puja any more. There was no need to appease the goddess of crops. Why offer her anything when you didn't need to grow anything in her land? That didn't mean the day wasn't celebrated, of course. It was, in fact, celebrated with great fanfare much like Deepavali and Pongal – with brand new clothes, gold jewellery, new vehicles, film releases, and a feast the day after with mutton and chicken bought from the town butcher.

Subbiah was puzzled that his wife hadn't brought the offerings herself but he soon concluded that something must be keeping her busy and did not give it much thought. She was a lover of tilled earth like him, a woman who had never wished for anything other than the simple life of a farmer's wife. She spent many a night with him by the shed. Scarecrow couple, they were called but neither of them minded it. They loved the crops as much as they loved their children, if not more. He and Rukkamma hadn't spoken more than a few words to each other in years; what was left to speak after a point? They worked together in the fields, side by side, every day. He wasn't interested in listening to household issues and she never bothered him with them. He wanted to be left alone – to sow, to water the cane, to pull out the weeds, to plough the land, to watch the paddy grow. It was his life. He didn't know if they made any money from the land. That wasn't his business.

As he spread the plantain leaf on the ground and tidily arranged the rice and pongal on it, he wished for a moment that the whole family was there for the ceremony even though he knew that was not to be. His brother Thirumalai came only for harvests, his sister-in-law hadn't visited the farm in decades and the younger generation had better things to do, he was told. He tied a towel around his hips over his dhoti, and was about to start the puja when he heard his grandson in the distance.

'Thatha, I'm coming, please wait for me.' Subbiah smiled and waited for Vijay. The boy ran the last hundred metres and stopped in front of his grandfather, panting.

'But where's paatti?' he demanded.

~

'They say it's the New Year but your family doesn't seem to know it. They haven't sent anything. What have they ever given you?' Sundaram taunted his wife, bright and early.

'Oh, shut up,' Vasanta snapped. 'You destroyed all we had and now you complain about my family.'

'Everyone knows what goes on in your family. Your father's brother and his wife suck the family wealth, and treat your parents like farm labour. But what do *they* do? Give up their own home and sleep in the fields! Let me ask you this, does your father think he is Jesus Christ?' Sundaram asked.

Vasanta did not bother to reply because she knew he wouldn't give up and because there was more than an inkling of truth in what he said. She and her brother had grown up like orphans in their large family home. Their parents, lovers of the earth, toiled in the fields all day oblivious to everything else, while they were left to fend for themselves at home. What chance did they have against their all-powerful aunt? Vasanta, as a young girl, ended up with most of the house work, and had had to stop her studies midway to help with the household chores. She was married off young to the good-for-nothing Sundaram with almost no gold except what her mother had received from her family.

'When are we getting the land they owe us?' Sundaram continued, emboldened by Vasanta's silence. Vasanta's eyes flashed as she got up and went inside the house. Much as she hated to admit it, her husband was right. They had got nothing from the family wealth. She had not complained all these years but now she had overwhelming needs – two sons in college, Sundaram's medical expenses – and it was too much for her to manage. Fortunately, her eldest had started working and he was saving money to build a proper house. Her parents' family owned nearly half the village land and, goaded by her husband, she had asked her uncle Thirumalai, her father's elder brother, for a few cents of land to build a house. He had refused, and in the same week he had bought a house in town for his own daughter, Vasanta's cousin.

Enraged by the injustice, she had taken out her frustration on her poor mother a couple of days ago and told her that she wasn't welcome unless she spoke to her brother-in-law about the land. Rukkamma, who had never fought for anything in life, left discomfited and confused, clueless as to how to claim an insignificant portion of her rightful share for her daughter. Vasanta had not seen her mother since then, and was feeling guilty for having unduly pushed the plain-hearted old woman. It was the New Year, after all. She should go over to the family mansion and ask for blessings from her. She was about to leave when her young nephew Vijay came running inside the house.

'Is paatti here?' he asked. 'She's not in the farm.'

~

Thirumalai reclined in the easy chair, watching television as every channel aired special programmes on the day. On Sun TV, a young woman from the city was visiting a village to show her viewers how the occasion is celebrated traditionally. A man with a plough was smiling idiotically on camera, standing next to the host.

'Made up news as usual,' Thirumalai mumbled and changed channels. He didn't believe that there were still backward villages in the state where people went to the fields and ploughed early to celebrate the New Year. Even if they wanted to do it, where would they get labour from?

'Jaggery, she wants now! Does she know how much a kilo of jaggery costs?' Poomathi, his wife, ambled over to where he sat, jingling the key ring tied to the new sari that he had bought her for the New Year. She sat down next to his chair.

'Who wants jaggery?'

'Lalitha, she wanted a kilo from the store,' she said, referring to the youngest daughter-in-law of the house. Not hers, of course. Lalitha was married to Maran, the only son of Subbiah and Rukkamma. The poor girl had come into the house thinking dealing with gentle Rukkamma would be fairly easy and it was, but she hadn't known then that the real power in the household was vested in the terror that was Poomathi, wife of Thirumalai, the patriarch of the family.

'She said she wants to make sweet pongal for the evening,' Poomathi continued. 'Her husband loves it. I told her with all the money her husband and father-in-law earn, they can't afford sweet pongal.'

'That is true. But it's New Year. Perhaps...' Thirumalai had a sweet tooth, along with diabetes, and he loved Lalitha's cooking. Her sweet pongal was worth dying for.

'This is why they think they can get away with anything. You give in too easily. What have they done for the family? You take care of everything, they are wealth-destroyers, all of them. But you want to give away everything to them!' Poomathi started her tirade.

'True but my brother and his wife work in the farm...'

'Work! Is that what you think they do? She goes and stays in the shed on most nights too. Shameless at this age! And you so naive, they do work indeed. I brought up her two children like my own while she was frolicking in the fields and everyone knows it.'

Thirumalai did not say anything. He knew everyone

thought quite differently about how Vasanta and Maran were brought up but it was best not to talk when Poomathi was in this frame of mind.

'Do you know what that woman asked me the other day? You would fall out of your chair if you knew.'

'What did she ask for?' he asked though he knew the answer. Rukkamma had come to him too.

'They want us to give land for Vasanta.'

'Land to Vasanta? For what?' Thirumalai looked appropriately shocked.

'To build a house supposedly. Doesn't she have a house of her own? Whoever gave land to women? And even if we did, what do we owe Vasanta and Maran? The bloodsuckers! Their parents have done nothing to contribute to the family wealth. Why do we have to give them anything?'

'Of course, we aren't going to give land to Vasanta. Sacrilege!'

'That woman won't ask again as I've shut her mouth quite effectively. I asked what was it that she brought from her father that she now thinks we should give land to Vasanta. She didn't say a word after that…and here comes the third-generation pest!'

'Paatti!' Vijay was running towards them like a jallikattu bull. Poomathi stepped aside to avoid the collision.

'Rukku paatti has disappeared!'

~

Soon, the search for Rukkamma was on all over Ayyanarpatti. Men were dispatched to far-off fields to look for the missing grandmother. Special attention was paid to wells, at least the few that weren't entirely dry yet. No one had seen her since the night before. Rukkamma was known to be fond of visiting relatives in near and distant villages, but she always took someone along for company. Rukkamma had never gone outside Ayyanarpatti by herself. The woman was hardly literate. Where could she go?

By afternoon, the village elders called on Thirumalai and, after a lengthy and intense discussion, suggested that he summon a priest to see if he could see her in his far-reaching vision. A few of the young men, on the other hand, wanted to inform the police but Thirumalai ruled that out sternly. Whoever heard of calling the police to report a missing person? This was a village issue, and the family honour would be lost if police entered the ancestral house. Through the afternoon, as everyone was discussing his wife's disappearance, Subbiah sat in the thinnai by himself, a little worried but mostly perplexed.

The call from Maruthappan, Rukkamma's cousin once removed, came early evening. Rukkamma was in Sirungudi, her childhood home, and she was safe and sound. Yes, she had taken bus no. 22 to get there and, as far as he knew, she had travelled by herself. She was resting and wasn't available to speak on the phone. Thirumalai cursed his sister-in-law and informed Maruthappan that someone would be there in the next couple of days to accompany her back. Maruthappan assured him that there was no hurry and they were more than happy to host her. The search was called off and villagers went back home to their television sets for continued entertainment.

'That woman's nerve! How could she go by without telling anyone?' Poomathi asked her husband. 'And now you have to drop all the work here and fetch her from that godforsaken village.'

Subbiah cleared his throat but, as usual, he was ignored. After hanging around for a while, he left for the farm shed. Rukkamma would be fine, she could take care of herself, but the crops needed him.

~

A week later, Thirumalai alighted bus no. 22 and walked along the uneven road towards the village of Sirungudi. He had wanted to take his moped but it was too far and he was too old to be gallivanting around on a motorcycle. Besides, he couldn't bring back his sister-in-law on the TVS XL. Poomathi would not approve.

He remembered the first time he had visited Sirungudi nearly forty years ago, travelling by the same bus. He had come to the village regarding a marriage proposal for his younger brother Subbiah. His brother did not come with them as he was to be the groom. Thirumalai had come to see young Rukkamma with his parents and his still-new wife Poomathi. Rukkamma was an unusually beautiful girl – tall, with well-rounded hips, fair, with the face of a full moon. He was intensely jealous of the good fortune that was going to befall his simple brother. He tried his best to discourage his parents from going ahead but his father stood firm, and Subbiah married Rukkamma. Since the day of that wedding forty years ago, Thirumalai was forced to steal lecherous glances in his sister-in-law's direction knowing fully well that any advances would be firmly rejected.

So long ago, and he still couldn't get over his brother's good fortune. He was careful not to show any outward sign of his illicit attraction for his sister-in-law. Appearances mattered, but more than that it was the thought of his wife's wrath that kept him at bay. Outwardly, he was often rude to Rukkamma, or ignored her presence altogether. However, a few days ago, the woman had come to him for help. It was the first time she had approached him for a favour. She hesitantly asked him if he could gift some land for Vasanta to build a house.

'Over my dead body,' he'd laughed.

Nevertheless, since then, over the past few days, he had been rethinking the decision. He was well aware that villagers gossiped about the way he treated his brother and family. They said he only cared for his own children but, well, why shouldn't he? They were, after all, his own progeny. The responsibility of taking care of the joint family fell on his shoulders when his father passed away and he had performed the task to the best of his ability. If his children came out better because of it, why hold that against him? He knew that wasn't how the world saw it, and as he grew old, he was vain enough to want to change their opinion of him. Legacy had started mattering to him lately and he had almost made up his mind to give in and offer Vasanta the land behind the old haystack. They had no use for it and it wouldn't fetch much in the market. He still had to convince his wife, and that was no ordinary task.

'Anna! Come in please,' Maruthappan invited him inside. 'Rukku, see who is here,' he called out.

Thirumalai sat down in the thinnai and enquired after the family and everyone else he knew in Sirungudi. Maruthappan's wife brought him extra-sweet tea and laddoos, which he ate heartily. Rukkamma had not made an appearance yet and Thirumalai naturally assumed that she was packing and getting ready for the journey back to Ayyanarpatti.

'We ought to be leaving soon,' he said, as the conversation lulled.

'Oh, I think Rukkamma would like to stay here for a while,' Maruthappan informed him with a disarming smile. Thirumalai was taken aback. Did he hear this man say that he wouldn't be allowed to take back a woman who belonged to his family?

'But…why? Everyone's missing her back home. She can visit you some other time,' he said, flashing a wide smile himself.

'Well, you know she hasn't spent much time here in decades, and so she wants to stay on longer. She says she wants to do work on her father's house and restore it,' Maruthappan explained. Rukkamma was his uncle's only child and they had been close growing up. He was glad that she wanted to spend time at his home, and so were his children. Rukkamma's father's lands were being tilled by his family though technically she was the rightful heir. Rukkamma was more than welcome in Maruthappan's household, and if she wanted to stay, she would stay. He wasn't going to send her away with Thirumalai.

'I don't think that will do at all. There is a lot of farm work that needs to happen and we can't really do without Rukkamma.' Thirumalai decided to be firm. It wouldn't do to give in to these people. If you let them, they'd climb on your head and start peeing, he told himself.

'Is that so? Can't your household with all your wealth afford a farm labourer that you need a sixty-year-old woman to do the work?'

Thirumalai looked up at Maruthappan in disbelief. Did he hear that right? Maruthappan still had that idiotic smile that was in total contrast to what he was saying. Thirumalai stood up. He had to have a talk with her; there was no use in talking to her relatives.

'I would like to speak to Rukkamma. Please call her.'

Rukkamma, who had been waiting behind the door all this while, came forward and stood in front of the door, her eyes firmly on the floor.

'Pack your things. I came all the way for you.'

'I'll stay here for a while,' she replied, looking as demure as when she had offered him tea forty years earlier when he had come about the marriage proposal.

'But everyone at home… Vasanta and Maran and…'

'They'll be fine without me.'

'But why do you want to stay here?'

'I like it here. I grew up here.'

'This is not your home.'

Rukkamma did not reply.

'Don't think this drama will make us give land to Vasanta! In fact, I am all the more determined now. She will not get a cent.'

Rukkamma turned around and walked towards the courtyard without saying another word. Thirumalai left Sirungudi, furious and defeated.

~

When Vasanta came to visit her mother a few days later, Rukkamma had all but moved to her father's old house. Vasanta felt terrible as she was certain that she had caused her mother to leave Ayyanarpatti. She begged for forgiveness but Rukkamma assured her that there was nothing to forgive. She hadn't run away because of her daughter. Vasanta beseeched her mother to come back; her pleas were useless. Rukkamma invited her and the children to visit her as often as they liked but was firm that she wasn't coming back to Ayyanarpatti. She was at home in Sirungudi.

Maran and Lalitha came next. Maran hadn't spoken to his mother in years and he just stood there nudging his wife. After a few minutes, Lalitha quietly asked him to leave them alone and he left, feeling relieved. Lalitha then spent an enjoyable couple of hours with her mother-in-law telling her of all the happenings back in the village. Apparently Sundaram had started building in the land behind the haystack without permission from Thirumalai and there was a huge uproar. Poomathi, on hearing the news, took a broomstick and rushed to the disputed land and had to be forcibly brought back home. She was even more spiteful than before but Lalitha knew how best to take care of herself. She had no intention of requesting Rukkamma to come back. She was glad that unlike herself Rukkamma had a place to go to, a place to call home. When Maran came back, she told him that despite her best attempts, his mother wouldn't be coming back to Ayyanarpatti.

A steady stream of visitors from Ayyanarpatti came to Sirungudi over the next several days to convince Rukkamma to come back home. It seemed that people who had never noticed her presence all these years were missing her and wanted her to come back to what they claimed was her rightful home. Rukkamma didn't know what to do with all the attention she was getting but she was old enough to know it was fleeting.

Finally, weeks later, one day, when she was in the field talking to a young coconut palm on the embankment, she saw a familiar hunched figure in the distance. She smiled and waved. Subbiah walked towards her and sat down on the embankment.

'Sit down,' he told her, clearing away the twigs to make space for her. Rukkamma sat down obediently.

'How are you?' he enquired.

'I am well. How have you been?'

'We finished harvesting cane last week. I couldn't leave before that.' He was apologetic, but not more than usual.

'Of course. How did it go?'

'It took weeks to get the men to turn up but it's okay now. We are done,' he replied. Husband and wife silently watched the women pull out weeds from the field.

'Are you happy here?' he asked.

'Yes, this land was my father's, now mine. I am happy,' she replied.

Subbiah looked sad but nodded his head. 'Do you sleep

in that shed?' he asked pointing to a shed in the distance. 'You have to be careful.'

Rukkamma laughed. 'No, one of my nephews is the scarecrow here. I go back to the house in the evening. How's the groundnut coming along?'

'Not like the old days but it's growing and I haven't given up yet. I think it'll survive and if there's a good yield, next season, I'll sow sesame.'

'You should let me know how that turns out.'

'You can come see for yourself,' he said, hopeful.

'I don't know. Will you visit me?'

There was the answer. He would have to learn to live with it.

'Yes,' he said simply. 'I'll come after the paddy harvest.'

'I'll be expecting you.'

Subbiah smiled and got up to leave.

'Please have dinner with me,' she said, surprising herself.

'I'll miss the bus if I stay longer.'

'You can leave in the morning,' Rukkamma giggled. 'If you miss your shed, we can sleep in this one tonight.'

Subbiah laughed and sat back down on the embankment.

The Amman of Saris

Vaikasi in Ayyanarpatti has become synonymous with the Kamakshi Amman festival in recent times. Until a few years ago, the Kamakshi Amman used to be an unknown deity in these parts but that changed when one fine day a benefactor arrived from the city in search of a goddess by a lake he had seen in a dream. The man's chauffeur, an astute young man as it turned out, led his employer to the temple in his native village, and pointed out the similarities between Kamakshi and the goddess who appeared in the dream. Convinced or perhaps conscious that the driver in question was his benami in a number of questionable business transactions back in the city, the rich man decided to rebuild the dilapidated temple, and since then the rebirth of the goddess is celebrated every Vaikasi with much fanfare. Devotees and visitors from towns and villages in the district flock to Ayyanarpatti for the week-long celebrations that culminate in a grand puja on the night of the full moon.

But this year, the arrival of the auspicious and usually profitable month did nothing to lift Ramu's flagging spirits. The ageing proprietor of Kalyani Textiles in Rayavaram town was perusing the day's *Daily Post* from his usual spot behind the cash counter.

'Sivannur temple celebrates motherhood – hundreds of sons and daughters pay homage to their mothers with sovereign gifts and special offerings.'

He continued reading but the news didn't register as his real attention was taken up by the steady stream of customers in Manian's flower stall across the street. By last count, thirty-seven customers had visited the flower vendor since the morning compared to his two. Ramu wistfully wished he had a flower business; there was always a demand for flowers. Girls bought flowers to adorn their hair on the way to college in the morning; men picked up flowers for their wives every evening irrespective of the season; devotees took them to temples daily to placate the gods; every week there was a political meeting for which flower garlands were a must-have; and all this in addition to the exorbitant amount of flowers used in weddings and other celebrations.

It definitely was a lucrative business, Ramu concluded glumly, unlike textiles where he had enormous set-up costs and was stuck with lakhs of unsold inventory in a bad year. And there was no question that he had had a bad year. The worldwide recession had finally reached his showroom via Singapore and the Middle East. Due to the scarcity of new jobs and increased visa restrictions, very few of the migrant boys came back for annual visits, and the ones who came back returned for good. In a region where every other household had at least one earning member in these countries, it meant that discretionary spending was at an all-time low.

'Not for Manian,' Ramu cursed his luck as the thirty-eighth customer entered the flower stall. The festival had clearly arrived early for the flower vendor.

Ramu folded the newspaper and put it down on the table. His eyes fell on the bundle of new saris that had arrived from Calcutta the day before. The saris were plain white with red or black borders, like a widow's. No woman in her right mind would buy them. He shouldn't have let Rajesh go by himself and choose the merchandise. His nearly middle-aged son was useless at most things including the family business. There he was now, chatting up one of the new shop girls! That he was very good at.

'Rajesh, who is going to buy these saris?' he demanded.

'They are very popular in Calcutta,' his son replied nonchalantly. He pointed them out to the shop girl. 'Don't you like them?' he asked her.

'Why, is Calcutta full of widows?' Ramu asked his son.

'Don't worry, appa. I'll sell them.'

'How? Are you going to murder all married men in the district?'

Rajesh did not bother to reply. In his opinion, his father was only good for sitting behind the counter and collecting cash from customers. Silly old man! He would show him how to sell saris.

'Chandran anna, Vasanti akka, how are you?' He smiled invitingly at the two prospective customers from his village who had entered the showroom. 'Are you looking for Kamakshi saris today?'

Vasanti's eyes narrowed. 'What are those?' she enquired.

'Oh no, don't ask him. They come up with new names

for old saris every month!' Chandran whispered but his wife wasn't used to paying him much attention.

'What? You haven't heard of the Kamakshi sari? Everyone is buying them for the festival and we are running out of stock!' Rajesh exclaimed. Ramu raised his eyebrows and stealthily looked at his son, who ignored him.

'Here, look at them.' Rajesh walked over to the box of new saris, pulled the top one out and spread it open on the counter.

Vasanti felt its texture and looked up at him, puzzled. 'What is special about this sari?'

'This particular type of sari is a gift from Vishnu, the goddess's brother. All men are to buy the saris for their sisters, and have the saris blessed by Kamakshi Amman before handing them over to their sisters. In fact, I'd be surprised if your brothers haven't already bought yours, akka,' Rajesh explained.

Ramu slowly unfolded the newspaper and reread the news article on the festival in Sivannur, the one where mothers were honoured. There was an unmistakable similarity between the news story and the one his son had just narrated, and he looked at Rajesh in shock.

Chandran had a frown on his face but he did not dare interfere in the conversation. After all, he had no sisters while his wife had three male siblings.

'You are right. I am sure they'd have bought saris already.' Vasanti nudged her husband.

'If I were you, I wouldn't be so confident of that. They are—'

Vasanti shot Chandran a sharp look and he stopped

in mid-sentence. She took the sari from Rajesh and held it against her. 'But…why are they white? Isn't white the colour of…?'

'Not at all. White is Kamakshi's favourite colour. The great man who rebuilt our temple – he said that the goddess was wearing white in his dream, don't you remember?'

'Of course. How could I've forgotten?'

'White with a red or black border. It was a hazy dream.' Rajesh pushed his luck but it held firm.

'What if the woman has more than one brother?' Vasanti raised a pertinent question.

'Each of your brothers has to buy a separate one. Otherwise they wouldn't be blessed,' Rajesh answered confidently. He knew what he was talking about – making it up as he went along. Vasanti nodded sagely. Husband and wife left the shop soon after, having forgotten what they had originally come to buy.

Before long, every adult male in the district who was unfortunate enough to have a sister was buying Kamakshi saris. A few more details were added to the story such as that of Kamakshi being a militant goddess who wouldn't hesitate to cut down brothers who did not cherish their sisters. Brother-less women felt left out until someone decided that the fathers were a good stand-in and could buy them the saris instead. Kalyani Textiles received calls from far-flung villages asking for Kamakshi saris. Rajesh had to order a few more shipments, some of which he sold wholesale to other retailers. He didn't want to be the only vendor selling Kamakshi saris in town.

A few days before the festival, a reluctant Ramu, nudged

by Rajesh, went to meet the temple's chief priest, a few specially chosen saris in hand. One of them was for the goddess, and the rest for the priest's sisters. The priest swore to Ramu that the goddess herself had appeared to him in his dream demanding a sari puja along with the regular offerings, and he promised Ramu that his generosity would be explained explicitly to her as part of the puja. Following advice from the priest, the Kamakshi saris had to be dropped in a special tent set up near the temple for this purpose. The saris would be offered to the goddess during the full moon puja after which brothers were free to distribute them to their respective siblings.

~

The evening of the festival found Ramu cloistered in the prayer room of his spacious house in Upper Street, Ayyanarpatti. His brothers had left early for the temple as the family was playing a prominent part in the puja but Ramu was busy apologizing to the gods at home one last time. He begged forgiveness not only for his son's deception but also for his own impudence in reminding them that the deception was for a good cause. Men did not look after their sisters like they used to in his days, and it was surely not an unforgivable sin for his son to try to rectify that, however unconventional the approach may be. He asked the gods to give him a sign, before the day was over, that all was forgiven, and stepped out into the courtyard.

A girl, one of his many granddaughters, was carefully applying kajal to her eyes with one hand, holding a small mirror in her other hand; her mother was adjusting her sari for the umpteenth time; another granddaughter was piling on oodles of Fair & Lovely on her face in an attempt to look fairer. A couple of older women were edging each other out in front of the wall-length mirror trying to get one last look before they stepped out of the house. There were about half a dozen baskets filled with paddy and rice grains on the narrow table next to the mirror. A few garlands of various sizes hung from the wooden ceiling and two large plantain clusters leaned against one of the wooden pillars around the courtyard. In one corner, a young girl was sitting next to the windowsill, her drawing book open in front of her. Ramu walked towards the girl – his favourite grandchild, a visitor from the city.

'I am not coming to the temple,' Leela informed her bemused mother, who was standing next to her, hands on her hips.

'Darling, you come with me, we can sit in the front and see everything,' Ramu, who had overheard her, told her gently.

'Listen to your grandfather. We came to the village for this festival,' Karpagam reasoned with her eight-year-old though she knew that this was likely to be a losing battle. Little Leela had a reputation for getting her way.

'I didn't want to come to the village. You wanted to come here, so you go to the festival,' Leela retorted. She smiled sweetly at Ramu. 'I want to draw.' She put her pencil to paper and started scribbling.

'Bring your book and you can draw in the temple. You'll have lots of things to draw – the goddess, the puja, the kavadi for Murugan. You can sit next to me, right in front of the goddess.'

Leela firmly shook her head and continued to draw. Ramu sighed and turned to his daughter. 'Let her stay if she wants to.'

'Appa! What are you doing here with the womenfolk? They are searching for you in the temple.' It was Rajesh, who had come back to the house to goad the stragglers. Ramu left the house hurriedly. It wouldn't do to keep the goddess waiting. Not when he desperately needed the Amman to forgive him.

'How long will you women take to get ready? The goddess can't wait for you to finish your make-up. Let's go. Now!' Rajesh shouted and clapped his hands.

'Call one of the men to carry the plantain, we'll bring the rest,' Karpagam told her brother.

'I'll carry them myself.'

'You'll stain your new clothes. Get one of the farmhands.'

'Don't worry, my dear wife will wash them with her lovely hands if they get stained,' he said as he lifted the plantain clusters. He swung them over his shoulders and strutted out. The rest of them followed, with rice, paddy and the garlands.

'Leela, you ought to come.' Karpagam tried one last time. Leela ignored her and continued to draw. Karpagam turned around and left the courtyard without another word. Leela drew a picture of her uncle Rajesh and made him out to be a Bheema with his two gathas, except that in this case the gathas were plantain clusters. She held up her handiwork and admired it for a few moments. She looked around for new material when she realized that the house was empty and deathly quiet.

'Ah, now you wish you'd gone with your mother, don't you?'

Leela jumped. Indu, her older cousin, the country girl she usually ignored, was standing at the other end of the courtyard.

'No,' she replied. 'Why aren't you at the temple?'

'I have my periods, and the Amman doesn't like girls who have periods.'

'Doesn't the Amman get periods?'

'I don't know. But I'm going anyway.'

'You said you can't go.'

'I won't go into the inner sanctum. The goddess won't mind. You better come with me.'

'No.'

There was a sudden loud thud from outside the window. Leela looked around, frightened. She took a few steps back.

'Did you hear that?'

Indu nodded, the beginnings of a smile on her face. It was time someone gave her spoilt little city cousin a scare and she was feeling very much up to the job.

'What was that?' Leela demanded.

'All sorts of things happen in a village like ours. There are things that move about.'

'What things?'

'Have you seen ghosts?'

Leela laughed nervously. 'Ghosts don't exist.'

'Are you certain?'

Indu looked behind Leela at the window and started

walking towards it. They could now hear a scraping noise.

'Are you sure ghosts don't exist? Shall I open the window then?' She unlatched the window and opened it slowly. Leela cried out and ran to the other end of the courtyard and slipped inside a room. She could hear Indu's laughter echoing in the courtyard. Leela slowly peered through the door. Indu had her back to her but she could hear her clearly.

'Senthil, my cousin thinks you are a ghost!'

Senthil? Do ghosts have names? Even if they did, Senthil didn't really sound like a ghost's name. She stepped back into the yard. Indu was whispering now, and she couldn't make out what she was saying. She waited patiently until Indu had closed the window.

'Who's Senthil?'

'A ghost.'

'Is he your boyfriend?'

'Just a boy from school.'

'What did he want?'

'He came to say hello as he was in the village for the festival.' Indu didn't like this line of questioning but she answered all the same.

'Why didn't he knock on the front door?'

'I don't know.'

'Do you like him?'

'Yeah.'

'Then he is your boyfriend.' In Leela's mind, the last piece of the puzzle just slid into place.

'Don't talk nonsense. I am going to the festival.'

Leela shook her head. 'It's boring.'

'Have you seen people walk on fire? Kavadi bearers will carry their little palanquins and walk on fire to impress Murugan.'

'Walk on fire! Really?'

'Come see for yourself.'

Leela was clearly tempted and Indu pushed on. She was determined to take the younger girl with her – not just because she couldn't be left home alone but having Leela with her would help her case if she got into trouble. She told Leela both of them could go in disguise. She would go as a regular boy as she was skinny and tall, but Leela could go as someone more interesting.

'Would you like to be a kavadi bearer?'

Leela was reminded of the pictures on TV of young boys and girls dressed in yellow robes carrying little gods in a palanquin. Most had a spear, Murugan's vel, pierced from one cheek through the other.

'No!'

'Don't worry, you don't have to wear a spear. I'll dress you up in a small sari and paint your face. You'll have to carry two idols, one of Kamakshi and one of Murugan. I'll show you the palanquin.'

Indu went into the prayer room and brought out the small kavadi palanquin. Leela took it; it weighed nothing. This adventure sounded rather exciting. They would go to the festival in disguise and she would be a kavadi carrier. This outing was guaranteed to garner the attention of her friends in school who weren't really impressed when she told them she was going to Ayyanarpatti which was to them a village in the middle of nowhere.

Half an hour later, a well-dressed teenage boy sporting a budding moustache and an incongruous baseball cap left Ramu's house, followed by a young kavadi girl wearing a Kamakshi sari. The Kamakshi sari for young kavadi bearers was another one of Rajesh's coups of the past few weeks. The girl's face was painted red, and she had black liner dots above her eyebrows. She was carrying a small kavadi palanquin on her shoulder.

'We'll take a shortcut,' Indu said and grabbed Leela's hand. They cut through the old government well to get to the tamarind grove, at the end of which was the back entrance of the temple complex. As they neared the temple, they could hear the loudspeakers blaring, and had to shout over the din to be heard.

They were almost at the temple now and could see scores of people milling about. Indu pointed out the tents where food was being prepared. One of the men cleaning a rather large aluminium vat called out to Leela, asking her where her spear was. Leela walked faster and Indu laughed. She told the younger girl that they were going towards the temple tank. But Leela wanted to go to the inner sanctum and pray to the Amman. Indu didn't want to leave Leela alone though she'd promised Senthil that she would meet him by the temple tank. In any case, Leela would be a distraction. It was better to let her go see the goddess. She'd be fine. Nobody was going to kidnap a little kavadi bearer.

'All right, but come back to this lamp post. I'll be here in fifteen minutes, okay? I'll take you to the fire walk, don't go anywhere else,' Indu cautioned her and left.

Leela headed towards the sanctum and the jostling

crowd gave way as they saw a kavadi bearer. Inside the main compound, there was a prayer fire around which priests were chanting shlokas. On one side of the yard was a large tank filled with Kamakshi saris, boxed and numbered, waiting to be blessed. All around her, people were praying devoutly, hands together, heads bowed. Leela noticed her mother and the rest of the family sitting behind the chief priest. Leela started praying to the goddess but her wish list was complete in a matter of seconds. She was getting bored and decided to make her way back to the lamp post.

Indu wasn't at the lamp post but Leela wasn't concerned. She could see the lamps being lit in the lake, and she guessed Indu was running late. She started to walk towards the tank when she felt a hand on her shoulder. She turned around, startled.

'Hey, bring the kavadi to the Lord. This way, this way,' said the stranger, a woman in a yellow sari, an adult kavadi bearer.

'I am waiting for my akka…er…my anna,' she said.

'They'll come, you follow us,' the woman said, pointing to a group of boys and girls, similarly attired, with kavadis on their shoulders. Leela had run into a group of real kavadi bearers.

'You won't get lost with us. Here, Mala, hold this girl's hand,' said the woman. A girl of about fifteen grabbed Leela's hand and dragged her along with the rest of the crowd. Leela kept looking behind for Indu but she was nowhere to be seen.

A few moments later, Leela felt the temperature rising. They were in the middle of a large crowd but people quickly moved out of their way.

'There, look,' the girl called Mala pointed out to her. 'Are you afraid?'

Leela stared at the flaming hot coals a little further away. The fire walk! Finally!

'No, this is what I wanted to see,' she told Mala excitedly. She desperately wished she had her drawing stuff with her.

'Good. A lot of kids your age are afraid to walk. You know it won't hurt, don't you?'

Leela stopped dead in her tracks. She was in a long queue of real kavadi bearers waiting to walk on the hot coals! As she kept staring, a man in a yellow dhoti with a spear pierced through his cheeks ran over the coals, screaming.

'No, I am not part of this…' she started explaining.

Mala eyed her in puzzlement. 'Don't be afraid. Look at the next one,' she tried to calm Leela.

But Leela had seen enough. It was one thing to stare at the fire walkers, sketch them and show off to her friends at school. It was another thing to actually walk on fire. She shook her hand free of Mala's grasp and bolted straight for the sanctum.

'Amma!' she screamed as she ran.

'She is running away. Catch her,' Mala shouted. Mala and a couple of other women started running after poor Leela. As Leela crossed the lamp post, she saw Indu looking at her in alarm. Indu tried to block those chasing Leela but it was no use, so she started running along with them.

Leela ran into the sanctum but other than the roaring fire of the puja, there was not a soul around. The door to the inner sanctum was closed. Leela knew she didn't have much time before they caught up with her. She clambered up the tank filled with saris and jumped into it. She pulled the white covering sheet over her and held tight. Her stalkers followed her into the courtyard, trailed closely by Indu who was determined to find her cousin before the crazy kavadi women got to her.

'She's my cousin and I am telling you, she is not a real kavadi carrier,' Indu explained.

'You rascal, go away from here. Nobody asked you,' Mala shooed Indu away.

Leela held her breath and waited as the women walked around the yard. After what seemed like eternity, she heard them leave the compound but she dared not peek outside. She wasn't planning to leave the container until the kavadi women went back home. She settled in and pulled the saris around her.

Outside the tank, Indu walked around, puzzled. She had seen Leela run inside and she knew there was no other way out. She walked towards the inner sanctum where the Amman rests but the door was shut. Only priests were allowed inside. Had Leela managed to get inside? Indu was about to open the door when the temple bells rang out in unison. A second later, the door in front of her opened, revealing a dazzling Amman and two priests chanting mantras in front of her. She stepped back and ran towards the exit when she noticed a long procession coming her way led by priests, followed by a large crowd of devotees. Indu moved quickly to one side as she recognized her family leading the charge along with the priests. The bells stopped ringing.

'This is it, Swamy – the holy sari tank that our Amman wanted,' Ramu said respectfully to the high priest. He had been at the forefront of all the offerings made that evening, and he had prayed fervently to every single deity, major and minor, to bless and forgive him and his son. Amman, show the sinner some pity!

'Yes, yes.' The high priest started reciting shlokas while his assistant went around the tank nine times, lamp in hand. The two priests who were inside the inner sanctum came out and joined the proceedings.

'The goddess has blessed the tank. Let us be thankful and receive her blessings,' the priest proclaimed finally and pulled the white sheet off the tank. He climbed on the stone step to take the first sari out, the one meant for the Amman. To his surprise, wrapped in the Amman's own sari, he saw a girl, her eyes tightly shut, the kavadi palanquin in her hand. He stepped back in alarm but recovered his composure quickly.

'Amman has given us a little girl,' he said slowly to the expectant crowd.

'It must be Kamakshi herself,' someone said and the temple bells rang out in agreement.

A little Kamakshi? This was the sign he had been asking for! The little Devi would tell him how to get back into her good graces, Ramu decided as he climbed up the steps. The goddess had listened to his prayers. He was indeed blessed! He looked inside the tank.

'Leela!' he exclaimed and lifted his granddaughter from the tank. She clung to him and kept on whispering 'I don't want to walk on fire.' Karpagam tried to make her way to the front but the crowd would not part. Everyone wanted to see Kamakshi's child.

'Please, it's my daughter. I have to take her home.'

'She's not your daughter! You can't take her home.'

'Is this girl from your household?' the priest enquired.

Ramu nodded, confounded. What was the Amman trying to tell him?

'This is a rebirth. She may be the goddess herself. Bring her inside the sanctum, come with me.'

Ramu followed the priest to the sanctum. Hands reached out from everywhere to touch the little Devi and get her blessings. Leela held on to her grandfather in fright but Ramu was oblivious; he was in a trance. The goddess was showing him the way and he was going to do as she bid him to. If his Leela was to be the little Devi, there was nothing he could do about it.

One of the assistant priests had laid down a mat in front of the fire. Ramu sat down, with Leela clinging tight to his shoulders.

'Fire! I don't want to walk on fire!' Leela started crying in earnest.

'Hush, little Devi,' the priest told her and he put his fingers to his lips.

Leela stopped crying but looked around frantically for her mother. 'Amma!'

'Of course, she wants her mother. Let her stay here tonight with Kamakshi. This is her home.'

'No!' Karpagam had finally managed to break through the crowd. She gathered up Leela in her arms. Ramu looked bewildered.

'Put her down!'

'The goddess has given her to us. She is our new Devi.'

'No,' Rajesh interjected. 'She's had a fright, we are taking her home.' He had been at the food tent 'supervising' and having a quick meal when Indu turned up to alert him. He knew this situation would get out of hand if it wasn't handled right. Karpagam turned and tried to walk towards the exit but no one gave way.

'The Amman has first rights over her.'

'Take her to the goddess.'

Karpagam looked at her brother in alarm.

'Please, my niece was at home and we have to find out what happened. Once we…'

'There is nothing to find out. The goddess brought her here and we have to let her stay here!'

'You!' Ramu suddenly shouted at his son. He seemed to have woken up from his trance. 'This is all your fault. You godless bastard—'

'Hush! All of you, listen to me.' Rajesh raised his voice.

'Why should we listen to you? We want to listen to her, the Devi!'

'Let her talk.'

'She may be able to predict our future.'

'No, no, I know what this means. The goddess came to me in my dream last night…'

'Liar!'

'Just hear me out,' Rajesh pleaded. 'This is a sign and I know what this means!'

'Godless liar. Go away.'

Rajesh grabbed a loudspeaker from one of the assistant priests and shouted into it.

'THE SARIS, THE KAMAKSHI SARIS ARE FREE!'

The crowd went silent for a moment as they pondered this new development.

'We will refund every single paise. That is what the Amman wants. This is why she brought our little girl from our home to the sari tank. This is the sign from my dream. Thank you Kamakshi for showing me the way!'

He dropped the loudspeaker and prostrated in front of the sanctum. Ramu fainted. Before anyone else could react, Karpagam started walking and this time the crowd parted to give her way. She walked all the way home, Leela in her arms, Indu following a step behind.

When the rest of the family arrived later at night, Leela was tucked in, fast asleep, with Karpagam keeping vigil, just in case. Indu, penitent, spent a restless night locked up in her room pretending to study. Ramu, revived, spent the night cursing his luck and his son. Rajesh didn't turn up home until the next morning. He had spent the night in the mango grove drinking, and he was careful to stay out of his father's sight for the next several weeks.

A Yank in Ayyanarpatti

'Where is this place again?' Meenakshi drawled, taking in a large mouthful of rum and Coke before placing the empty glass on the tray that magically made an appearance perched atop a waiter's outstretched palm.

'Another one please.'

The waiter vanished as quickly as he had appeared, and Ben took another sip of the Glenfiddich – the 21 Year Old Gran Reserva – before replying to his girlfriend of three weeks.

'Southwest – of here.'

'You have been in this country long enough to know that we don't do maps.'

Ben was about to reply but he was interrupted by the microphone that sprang to life from the other side of the lounge. The brand quiz was about to begin, the girl announced. There were rules, of course.

Raise your hand if you know the answer and we'll ask you to speak.

Do not shout out the brand. That's a disqualification.

Adults aren't allowed to answer. Unless the question passes to the audience.

'You don't have to subject yourself to this. We can go back to the flat,' Meenakshi said, holding a newly filled glass of rum and Coke.

'I don't mind. I can deal with building parties.'

About a dozen kids were gathered around the girl with the microphone. The handful of stragglers in the participant age group were being literally pushed by their parents to go to the front of the room and take part in the quiz. The first image went up on the screen – a horse on its hind legs. A number of hands shot up.

Ben shook his head. 'Who wouldn't know that?'

Ferrari

The next image looked like a coat of arms. A lion with a crown, a ship, a globe.

'I bet you don't know what that is.'

'I don't. Is it an Indian brand?'

'Nope. Only an American would ask that.'

Manchester United

'You are never going to get over the British, are you?'

'They are civilized compared to you.'

Ben did not reply. He was so used to the rest of the world calling him names that it didn't bother him any more. Another brand came up on the screen. Two branches around a globe. No hands shot up.

Ben chuckled. 'All right Ms Civilization, what is that *brand*?'

Meenakshi looked at the image, trying to remember where she'd seen it before. She shrugged. 'Something obscure. No one seems to know,' she said.

She was right. The question passed to the adult audience but no one in the room volunteered an answer.

'The United Nations,' Ben shouted and, without a backward glance, he opened the door to the balcony and let himself out. He needed fresh air, even the hot and humid air of steamy Chennai would do. Civilization indeed! Meenakshi followed him after a few seconds, her glass nearly empty.

'Trichy is the nearest city but there are a number of small towns near the village. The nearest one is Rayavaram,' Ben said, after a while.

Meenakshi looked at him, confused. 'Oh, the village. Will you be staying there?'

'I don't know yet. Rajkumar is sorting that out.'

Meenakshi made a face. 'Your driver is in charge of your accommodation?'

'Well, he knows the place better than I do. He says there are a lot of beautiful old mansions that can be rented for almost nothing.'

'He said they can be rented for almost nothing?'

'Not for him obviously.'

'I see. They have beautiful old mansions but they still need a white boy to build a simple house?'

'We are going to build the house in the village. The back story is that the man we are building it for belongs to a lower caste and they apparently still live in huts. Homes India, the NGO we are associated with, is helping them build quality homes and they roped us in since this would be a good way to prove our technology. We will know better once I am on the ground.'

'On the ground, the village belles will be out in full force. They will offer themselves up to you but the villagers will torch you for sleeping with someone of the wrong caste.'

'I don't have a caste.'

'It follows then whoever you sleep with will be of the wrong caste.'

Ben looked at her quizzically. 'I find it amazing how your impression of rural India is so much more exotic than mine. Have you ever been to a village?'

'No,' she said and turned away. They were both silent for a while, lost in their own thoughts. Ben was excited about the prospect of finally starting work on a real project but he was a tad apprehensive about working in a foreign, not to mention rural, setting where he did not know the language. Meenakshi wondered whether their relationship would outlast his project. She wasn't counting on it.

'Will you come visit?' he asked her.

Meenakshi looked up at him, incredulous. 'What would I do in a village?'

~

On a scorching hot Aani afternoon when most of Ayyanarpatti was still in the middle of their afternoon naps, Kuppan strode purposefully towards Balu's tea stall off Upper Street. There was a smattering of people about but no one acknowledged him. He was out of favour with the villagers since his attempted entry into the inner sanctum of the Kamakshi temple a couple of months ago. A pariah in the sanctum, they exclaimed! Who would have thought?

Kuppan and his family had been isolated from the village since that unforgivable transgression but Kuppan was unrepentant. He had been biding his time and now he was ready.

'One strong tea,' he told Balu as he sat down on an empty bench. Balu looked surprised but went behind the counter to pour out the tea. As long as he didn't speak to Kuppan, no one would find fault with him. Tea could be served in silence. Everyone knew you didn't refuse custom that came your way.

Kuppan looked around and away, and after a few moments pulled out his phone and stared at it expectantly. Balu served him tea in an aluminium tumbler. Kuppan's phone rang.

'Hello. Yes, this is Kuppan…Is Mr Ben coming too? I can arrange stay, no problem. You just come, sir. Everything's taken care of. Please tell Mr Ben that he can live in more comfort here than in America. Yes, yes, see you tomorrow.'

He hung up and sipped his tea. He was well aware that every eye in the tea stall was on him.

'Balu,' he asked innocently, 'do you know of any good mansions in town available for rent?'

Chandran guffawed from his usual place in the front bench. 'Why, your hut is in ruins that you are trading up to a mansion now?'

Kuppan smiled. Ah, so they do talk to him. 'Oh, not for me,' he said nonchalantly. 'I'm getting a new house built by Mr Ben who has come all the way from America just for this. I'm finding him a mansion to stay while he is here building my house. As I am sure you know, we can't really put him up in the village.' He got up from his seat and looked dismissively at the tea stall's clientele. 'Who in this village has a house fit for an American?'

Without waiting for a reply, he dropped a few coins on the counter and walked away, his shoulders erect and upright, his steps firm and measured.

Before the evening was out, everyone in Ayyanarpatti had heard of Kuppan's American builder. Some concluded that it was a hoax, while others thought Kuppan had gone mad since the sanctum episode. Goddess Kamakshi was taking her revenge. Or he must have won the lottery, someone said. Oh no, this is another government plan to steal from *us* and give to *them*. How much more are they entitled to? They have taken away our livelihoods, our women, and now this!

The news reached Builder Prasad's ears in Rayavaram late that night. A few months ago, Kuppan had approached him about building a new house. The old thatched-roof hut was coming apart and he needed a new home. Money wasn't an issue, two of Kuppan's sons were in Singapore and they sent money every month. But Builder Prasad didn't have time for Kuppan's house, or so he said. Labour was so hard to come by and he was focusing on bigger contracts, he explained. The reality was something quite different. Builder Prasad did not want to antagonize the relatively wealthy landowning community of Ayyanarpatti by building a house for Kuppan, a Dalit who wasn't in their good books. The bulk of Prasad's clientele came from neighbouring villages and reputation mattered in his profession. He was the undisputed builder in his corner of the world regardless of the fact that he did not possess a technical degree of any sort. But now, there was talk of this American builder who was coming to build Kuppan's house. He knew that the men from Homes India were talking to lower caste villagers but he didn't believe anything would come of it. It looked like he was wrong and it didn't bode well for his future. Builder Prasad needed to get to the bottom of this American builder business and nip it in the bud. Kali, his trusted lieutenant and driver, was urgently dispatched to Ayyanarpatti to keep an eye on the new arrivals.

~

The next day, Kali was sitting on a bench in the tea stall enjoying his unexpected holiday when the taxi, a white Indica, drove by. He quickly mounted his bicycle and followed the car up Upper Street. To his surprise, he wasn't the only one. A crowd was heading in the general direction of the Dalit colony outside the main village. As they got nearer, they could make out two men alight the taxi. One of them was a tall and well-built Dorai, a sahib, an American all right! The two men spoke to Kuppan though he had eyes only for Mr Ben. Soon, all three walked towards a piece of cleared land a couple of hundred yards away from Kuppan's hut. The driver of the taxi stepped out and leaned against it, lighting a cigarette. He sneered contemptuously at the gathering crowd.

Kali walked up to him. 'Is that sir going to build a house here?'

Rajkumar took a long drag before deigning to answer. 'Sir? Oh, you mean Ben. Yes, he's a builder.'

'Can't he find a job in his own country?'

The driver did not bother to reply to Kali's question.

'Is Kuppan paying him?' a villager enquired.

'How do I know? Ben has a company, an American company that has a stronger and cheaper construction technique. He'll finish the house in eight weeks,' the driver replied.

'Eight weeks!'

'Will he build houses for the rest of us?'

'How much does it cost?'

'Ben doesn't build for everyone,' the driver snapped.

That did nothing to placate a very worried Kali. The villagers were already starting to ask the American about prices. What will happen to his boss, Builder Prasad? He took off in his bicycle in a jiffy.

Meanwhile, the three men were coming back towards Kuppan's house. Ben was surprised to see so many people there while Kuppan was beaming.

'Idiots,' Vinay, Ben's operations manager, muttered under his breath. Kuppan, who had heard him, nodded his head. As they reached Kuppan's hut, they heard Chandran speaking to Rajkumar.

'Does he have a place to stay?'

'He's surely not going to stay in your old sorry home,' Kuppan replied sharply.

'But what about his food?' Chandran wanted to know.

'He wants beef every day – for breakfast, lunch and dinner. How many cows do you have in the village?' Vinay demanded. A shocked murmur went through the crowd. Ben, finally catching on that this was about him, looked enquiringly at Vinay. 'They want you to have food here. I told them you eat only beef.'

Ben looked shocked. 'No, no,' he tried explaining to Chandran. 'I don't want beef. I eat vegetables, fish and chicken.' He pointed to a group of cackling chicks in Kuppan's yard. Vinay and Rajkumar burst into laughter and the rest of the village followed. Ben looked around, puzzled, and then decided to join in.

~

Ayyanarpatti was a frenetic hub of activity the next few days. It took a couple of attempts before the new bore well started pumping out water. Specially made interlocking mud blocks were transported to the village, and a shed was built next to the site for the safekeeping of materials. Excavation began as soon as a small labour force arrived. Ben was initially astonished at the non-availability of local labour as, on any particular day, he saw able-bodied young men lounging about in Balu's tea stall. But he soon learned that they were in fact gainfully employed, by the government no less, as part of the rural employment guarantee scheme which was an effort to pay people for little or no work. This, combined with the Singapore remittances and the subsidized rice and assorted freebies, meant that there was no real incentive for anyone in the village to indulge in productive work, agricultural or otherwise.

Ben's labour situation was complicated by the fact that the builders in the region, Prasad prominent among them, were hoarding available masons, threatening them from joining the foreigner. Ben finally managed to procure labour from Vellore, thanks to Vinay's contacts, though most of the men were tribals from the north-east of the country and spoke little or no Tamil. The rumour went around the village that the labourers actually came from China, and had been sent here as part of China's plan for world domination. It didn't gain much currency with the majority of villagers who greeted them cheerfully enough.

Over the next few weeks, Ben settled into a regular routine. Rajkumar drove him from Rayavaram every morning – which Ben was beginning to see was inefficient and unnecessary as there were a number of buses on the route. Once he reached the village, he allocated the day's tasks to the masons and helped them with technical inputs. The villagers took turns in bringing him lunch though he wasn't able to convince anyone to take money for it. He found their hospitality endearing but overwhelming. After lunch, he took a few calls with investors and potential clients, followed by a check-in with Vinay, who managed a project near Chennai. He made an effort to help out on the site in the afternoon for the first few days but the scorching sun made him soon give up on the idea; he began taking a nap in the string cot under a shady neem tree next to Kuppan's house. He felt guilty about his nap until Meenakshi reminded him over the phone one day that only mad dogs and Englishmen go out in the midday sun. Well, he was neither and unlike his labour force, he had a choice. The men finished work early and wrapped up just as he woke up. He spent some time on site after the workers left, taking stock and making a list of tasks for the next day.

Evening tea was had at Balu's tea stall which he likened to taking an accelerated language course. He headed back to town after his tea and a couple of nights a week he had a few drinks with Rajkumar, Vinay and whoever happened to be around. He bought them Johnny Walker though when Vinay was around they had to be content with Mansion House. Vinay didn't believe in drinking with the lower classes and when forced to he frowned upon wasting good whisky on them.

On holidays and weekends, Rajkumar drove him back to Chennai. A night with Meenakshi and the expat crowd was intended to rejuvenate him and get him raring to go for the week ahead but as the weeks went by his trips became more infrequent. Meenakshi joked he had gone native but he knew it wasn't that. He was in India to get his hands dirty and build houses, and he'd rather spend his time doing that. Ben was content for the moment.

~

Three weeks later, the house was up to lintel level. Even the most sceptical of villagers were impressed by the progress on the house and there was a steady stream of interested visitors to see the house. Kuppan and his wife spent hours on the site showing people around, and updated their sons daily over the phone. Things were going as per schedule but Ben was worried. He was lying on the string cot under the neem tree as usual, his eyes shut, but he couldn't sleep. Someone was stealing building materials from the shed. A labourer had mentioned something about missing cement a few days ago but he hadn't paid much attention. Pilferage, to an extent, was fairly common on construction sites. But this time, it was two of the imported roof panels which were a core feature of the house. He had helped unload the panels a couple of days ago but two of them were gone as of this morning. He hadn't mentioned it to anyone yet but he'd have to inform Kuppan and ask him to keep a close watch on the shed at night.

Suddenly he heard a scraping noise above him and opened his eyes. Directly above him, a figure was sitting on a sturdy branch and chipping away at a nearby branch. The branch was about to fall on him! He quickly got up and moved away from the cot.

'Hey, you!'

A small leafy branch fell down next to the cot. He took a few steps backward and looked up the tree again. A tall, lanky girl was grinning down at him. She threw her garden knife on top of the branch and climbed down expertly as Ben watched in disbelief.

'You could have killed me!' he said, his hands making a cleaving movement across his neck. The girl ignored him and methodically gathered twigs and leaves from the fallen branch.

'What is it for?'

'My nephew has chicken pox. It's the season for it,' she answered in English.

'Oh.' Ben was perplexed. He could not fathom why she would gather neem leaves if her nephew had contracted chicken pox. Surely the right answer was to take him to a doctor. He vaguely remembered reading that in some parts of the world people believe that a goddess possessed you if you got chicken pox.

'Have you taken him to a doctor?'

Nithya scratched her chin and looked at him, disappointed. She had volunteered to fetch neem leaves because she was curious about Ben, the talk of the village these past few weeks. It wouldn't have been proper for her to show an interest, however innocent, in a young exhibit of the opposite sex, especially a western one since everyone knew they possessed neither culture nor morals. So she had been plotting hard to find a way of getting closer to Ben. To make things complicated, she had to catch him when his slimy driver wasn't around. The perfect opportunity seemed to present itself when Thiru fell ill with chicken pox and neem leaves had to be fetched from the Dalit colony for his bed as it would help relieve the itching. But this fool of an American did not seem to be worth all her effort. He thought they were so backward that they didn't take sick children to doctors.

'No, he doesn't need a doctor,' she said.

'But how will he get better? Is he taking any medication?'

'No. He'll get better soon. These leaves are all he needs.'

She tied her bundle of twigs and leaves with a string, heaved it over her shoulder and started walking towards the village, leaving Ben very concerned about her nephew. But he didn't have time to ponder over it as she quickly retraced her steps and untied her bundle. He looked at her, puzzled, until he saw a small delegation of villagers, all male, making their way towards Kuppan's house. When they reached the house, someone shouted for Kuppan to come out. Chandran, head of the delegation, noticed Nithya, who was busy pretending to gather leaves, and came forward. Ben smiled and was about to say something but Chandran ignored him altogether.

'What are you doing here?'

'Can't you see? Gathering neem leaves for Thiru.'

'You shouldn't have come here. Did you talk to him?'

'Of course not.'

Kuppan came out of the house and Chandran quickly walked back to join the crowd.

'What is going on?' Ben asked the girl.

'Sshhh.'

Nithya edged towards the crowd to hear better. They started talking in low voices but soon voices were raised. No one sat down on the benches in front of the house. It didn't look like Kuppan had invited them to. From what Ben could make out, Kuppan sounded angry and he was gesticulating wildly. After a while, the group hurried back towards the village. Kuppan stood in front of his house, seething.

'Please tell me what's happening,' he implored the girl.

'They want him to stop, they want you to stop building.'

'Why?'

'A number of bad omens have been seen in the village the past few days. Children have fallen ill. The most recent omen was the death of a cow yesterday.'

'What's that got to do with Kuppan's house?'

'They consulted a priest who said that this was because Kuppan has gone against the goddess's wishes in building a house and…'

'And?'

'And to make things worse, he has invited a foreigner to build it. They want him to stop immediately.'

'That's ridiculous.' He walked over to Kuppan and put his hand on Kuppan's shoulder. Kuppan jumped as if to defend himself but when he realized who it was he calmed down and smiled.

'No worries, Ben. You build the house,' he said and walked abruptly into the hut.

Ben turned to Nithya. 'What can they do if he goes ahead? It's his land, after all.'

'Isolate him, and refuse to work with him and his family. He went through it once when he entered the inner sanctum of the temple. His sons had to apologize and pay for a cleansing ceremony.'

'They can't do this!'

Nithya sighed. The stereotype she had heard about Americans being a bit slow was indeed true. 'Well, they told him he has to decide in two days.'

'I can step away from the project and let my colleague Vinay take over instead. I can talk to the village heads and make them understand. Who do I need to talk to?'

Nithya shook her head. 'It won't help.' She lifted her bundle and left.

~

Ben was on tenterhooks the rest of the day and he didn't sleep well. Early the next morning, he sent Rajkumar to Chennai to pick up Vinay; he didn't need the driver as he was planning to stay back in the village at night. He had decided to guard the materials shed himself. At the site, he shouted at the workers, which was out of character for him. He hardly ate any lunch and by mid-afternoon he was stretched out as usual on the cot. He sensed the girl approaching and kept his eyes half closed. She peered at him curiously before climbing up the neem tree.

'How is your nephew?' he asked, his eyes still shut.

Nithya almost lost her balance.

'It's got worse.'

'You should take him to a doctor.'

'That won't be necessary. We'll be taking him to the temple tonight to offer him up to the goddess.'

Ben was instantly up, eyes wide open. 'What do you mean offer him up?'

'We will take him to her, and if she wills it, she will take him back,' she said mysteriously as a branch fell next to Ben. She started climbing down.

'You should take him to a doctor immediately. If it is a question of money, I can…'

'Seeing a doctor is not expensive in our country.'

'They why don't you take him? Do you usually take them to the temple when they fall ill?'

'Only in cases when the pox is big and red. It is usually a sign that the goddess wants what's rightfully hers. You can come tonight to the temple to watch if you like. I'm gathering leaves because he'll have to lie down on a bed of neem when he is being offered.'

'But…but do you really believe that the goddess wants him back?'

'What's there not to believe?' she shrugged and changed the topic. 'Has Kuppan decided on the house?'

'Yes, he says he wants me to build it.'

'Has he spoken to his sons? They may think otherwise,' she cautioned.

'I don't know. Omens! These are just superstitions. How can you live your life like this?' Ben asked angrily.

Nithya struck her hand across her forehead. 'We live our lives the way we want to. Omens are convenient. They tell us what we want to see.'

Ben, buried in his frustration, didn't quite want to see and, as a result, he spent a rather disturbed evening. He went to the tea stall where Balu confirmed that some kids in the village had contracted chicken pox and that people were indeed gathering neem leaves for the beds of the sick. He also mentioned that special offerings were being made in the temple. Ben thought about calling Vinay and Meenakshi to ask them how he could stop this madness, but he knew that they wouldn't have a clue. He decided to go to the temple, and told himself over and over again that if things got out of control he'd do whatever he could to save the young lives.

Well past midnight, sitting in the outer sanctum of the Kamakshi temple, Ben started to feel stupid. The inner temple was locked and there was no sign of life. It was slowly dawning on him that he had been had. The girl had taken him for a ride and he had fallen for it hook, line and sinker. She had thrown enough clues but he was too dense. Feeling rather sheepish, he walked back towards the Dalit colony.

As he neared Kuppan's house, he saw a light coming from the site behind the shed. His pace quickened and he saw a flare go up heading for the roof of the shed. He started running, calling out for Kuppan as he ran. Kuppan came out just as a shape darted out from behind the shed and ran towards the bushes behind the neem tree. The shed was going up in flames. Ben was already at the bore well drawing water, and Kuppan ran over to help him. A scream rang out from the bushes but both Ben and Kuppan were busy dousing the fire. Kuppan's wife woke the neighbours and before long men and women were running towards the shed with buckets of water. The fire was out in a few minutes and both Kuppan and Ben spent the rest of the night in front of the shed.

Ben assessed the damage the next morning – one side of the shed had burnt down but most of the materials had escaped damage, including the roof panels. The half-constructed house was intact. Kuppan was on the phone to his sons in Singapore, and he was sobbing. Ben was relieved though, and he had started making the task list for the day when he saw Nithya and Kuppan's wife walking towards him. Nithya was carrying a long white cloth which looked like a bed sheet. Kuppan's wife ran to her husband waving a mobile phone. Kuppan immediately hung up and grabbed the phone from her.

'The arsonist's phone. It got stuck in the sheet when he tried to escape,' Nithya explained to Ben.

'That's brilliant...a sheet?'

Nithya looked embarrassed as she unfolded the sheet she was carrying. On a white bed sheet, there was a picture of Kali, gory and red, carrying a young boy's severed head.

'I had hung it up on the neem tree so that when you came back from the temple...' she began to explain. Ben started laughing and after a moment Nithya joined in as Kuppan and his wife stared at them in puzzlement.

~

After a few calls, the phone was traced to Kali, the driver and right-hand man of Builder Prasad of Rayavaram town. Ben wanted Kuppan to lodge a formal complaint but Kuppan laughed at the very idea of going to the police.

'You just build, Mr Ben. I'll take care of the rest,' he reassured him. He made sure that the news of Builder Prasad's treachery reached every village in the vicinity. His own village was the most difficult to convince but he had help from an unexpected quarter. It was that upper-caste girl who had found the phone and she was happy to tell everyone of her detective avatar. Once the situation was made clear, Kuppan was inundated with gifts and offers of help. No one spoke to him about stopping work on the house again. On the contrary, everyone enquired about the progress being made.

Ben stayed in Ayyanarpatti the rest of the month until the structure was complete. He had a project coming up near Madurai that required his attention, and he wasn't needed for the finishes. The villagers gave him a hero's goodbye – a feast with vegetables, fish, chicken and beef, the last specially procured from across the border.

Before starting work at Madurai, Ben went on a long

weekend trip to Bali with Meenakshi, who was glad to have him all to herself for a few days.

Nithya, despite her stellar investigative work, or perhaps because of it, was banned from visiting the Dalit colony. She did not approach Ben or speak to him during the rest of his stay in the village. She waited a few days after he had left before adding him on Facebook.

The Demon Wind of Aadi

Long, long ago, a dashing young hero on horseback carrying a top-secret missive for the emperor entered Chola country on the eighteenth day of Aadi but he was soon distracted from his mission by the overflowing lakes and reservoirs of the land and the festivities on the riverbanks. A modern-day Vandiyathevan, that endearing protagonist of the wildly popular Tamil historical tome *Ponniyin Selvan*, would still be able to witness the festivities of Aadi on riverbanks and in temples but the life-sustaining water which the month celebrates is in short supply since our present-day state and one of its neighbours have been fighting for the past several decades over who really owns the waters of the Kaveri. A hundred kilometres away from the Kaveri delta, in our little village of Ayyanarpatti, the water situation is even more dire as the land has to look up to the sky for deliverance, but Aadi is celebrated in much the same way.

Windy Aadi has the dubious distinction of being both an auspicious and an inauspicious month. Weddings cannot be conducted; new business ventures cannot be started; wives are advised to stay away from husbands during the month.

There are only two things that Aadi is meant for – festivals usually associated with water and the sowing of the year's paddy crop. In Ayyanarpatti, perennial cane also had to be harvested, making Aadi one of the busiest months of the year. Our villagers though spend the month rather leisurely in the various temples of the district praying to one goddess after another or in the shops in town buying saris and consumer appliances. (Aadi used to be the slowest month of the year as business sales went until enterprising entrepreneurs thought of Aadi discounts, making it a bumper month.) Half-hearted attempts were made at harvesting the cane and preparing the fields for sowing as the villagers waited for the old miller who owned a huge chunk of land across the district to find farmhands hoping that they could piggyback on him for their much smaller fields.

The sole exception to this indolent state of affairs was Natesan, Ayyanarpatti's self-made millionaire farmer, who had managed to harvest his cane crop as well as sow his paddy and as a result was sleeping soundly in his home on Upper Street.

'Tring...tring...'

Natesan woke up with a start at the jarring jingle of the bicycle bell. He switched on the light and looked up at the clock on the opposite wall. 5.10 a.m. It was too late for the milkman. Karuppiah would have milked the cows and left nearly an hour ago.

'Go back to sleep and I'll wake you up later,' his wife murmured. She slept on a blue-and-white coir mat on the floor next to Natesan's cot.

'No, I'm getting up now. I have to water the fields before we leave for the temple,' he said.

Raji turned around to look at him. 'The last load of cane was shipped yesterday. Get some rest.'

'I suppose it's cane that rises in your rice pot every day? There are acres out there which need to be watered. You ought to come to the fields and see for yourself.'

'While you cook for the farmhands? If I don't make food for them, we'll see who works in your fields.'

He started to reply but stopped himself and let Raji have the last word on this one. He got up, walked to the courtyard and looked around. His daughter's mat was neatly folded against the wall. 'Where's Kala?'

'She must have gone to the kollai. She'll start the motor pump and water the fields. Stop worrying,'

'Ah, it's her bicycle that I heard then. Good girl. The electricity schedule changes today and the pump has to be on early. Even if she is your daughter, she has sense!'

Raji pulled the sheet over her head and pretended to go back to sleep.

'Did Selva call?'

Selva was their teenage son who was away in a residential school in the city. Natesan had not spoken to him in a week as he had been busy with the farm. Raji pulled down her sheet slowly.

'He is not happy,' she said hesitantly.

Natesan frowned. 'What do you mean?'

'He has never stayed away from home even for a day,' Raji replied cautiously.

'So?'

'Poor child hasn't slept for even a single night since he went to the hostel. He's miserable. Can't he stay at home and go to school?'

Natesan looked at his wife angrily.

'At his age, I was beating metal. I pay a lot of money for him to study there and he complains? You can tell him that if he fails to act his age and get an engineering seat in a good college, he can come back and work as a farmhand.'

'Don't be upset,' Raji quickly reassured him. 'He'll get used to being there.'

'He better get used to it quickly. When are Kala's exams?'

'Next month. She needs money to pay the exam fees.'

'Ask her to get it from me before she leaves for college.' Natesan yawned and stretched his arms. 'I am going to write down accounts. I forgot to do that in the rush with the cane yesterday.'

Raji got up from her mat, rolled it around the pillow and pushed it to a corner. 'I'll make your tea,' she mumbled and ambled out of the room.

Natesan stood in his front yard, toothbrush in hand, and looked up at the neem tree. They were going to cut down the tree. He had managed all these years with trimming a few branches but now they wanted it gone. The lineman said that it was the only way for electricity to go to Vishwa's new house. Natesan did not agree. They could easily take it around the next street but the lineman was lazy and corrupt. He had probably submitted the plan for taking it through the long way, and put the extra money in his pocket. Maybe the assistant engineer was in it too. Who can trust these people? But Natesan couldn't afford to cross them. He needed to keep them happy for the line current in the fields. This tree had to go. It had been there all his life. He and his brothers had learnt to clean their teeth with its twigs. Its leaves covered and protected them when they fell ill one after another with chicken pox. The same way it protected both Kala and Selva when it was their turn. He shook his head and washed off the toothpaste under the government tap. He then climbed on the stone bench under the tree, reached up and broke a small branch. When Raji came out of the house with his tea, he was still trying to find the perfect twig.

Raji laughed. 'Ayye! You are brushing your teeth with a neem twig? Which century do you live in?'

'Oh yes, you are a Dorai's daughter, that's why you grew up brushing with a toothbrush.' Raji made a face, put the teacup down on the bench and hurried back into the house. Early morning was no time to have an argument. There was enough to do.

In a short while, Natesan followed her in with his tea. He pulled down the long accounts notebook from between the roof tiles in the courtyard and sat down on the floor. Most of the shopkeepers in Rayavaram town owed him money. A few of them were daily interest cases and if he didn't go into town to collect every day, they would default. Rascals! Why borrow money from him in the first place? He was a fair lender, not like that slimy PRC to whom they would have to pawn their lives. But fairness had lost its meaning, he told himself. Maybe usury was not for him. He was a farmer after all; he didn't have it in him to be a moneylender. He had assured his cousin Neru that he had cut back on daily interest lending. There were only a handful of daily collections now. Once he got the money back, he planned to stop daily lending altogether. When he started lending money after he came back from Singapore, he hadn't known of any other way to grow his money. But now there was land. He had already invested some money in real estate in nearby towns and perhaps he should do more of that. Everyone seemed to be making money from land these days.

'Tring…tring…' That bicycle bell again.

'Kala, is that you?'

'Yes, appa. I'm back from the kollai.' She parked her bicycle in front of the house and came inside.

'No sign of rain?'

'None whatsoever but the wind is crazy. I was nearly blown away.'

'Did you make sure that the coconut palms in the south end are getting water?'

'Yes, I had to divert the channel to get the water to reach the south end. Oh, I met Chelakannu anna on the way. His coconuts are gone again.'

'Impossible! He has a barbed wire fence. I saw it – it's strong and the points are razor sharp.'

'Looks like the monkeys have learnt to get around it somehow.'

'Monkeys!' Natesan exclaimed. 'They never used to come to the farmlands before. Now there is no Sengeerai forest and the monkeys and peacocks come to the fields and destroy everything. But this is Chelakannu's fault. I told him to electrify the fence leading up to the coconut palms. I even offered to split the cost when we were doing ours. He refused.'

'Oh! It's sad. This is the third time this year…appa, I have to pay the exam fee.'

'Get it before you go to the polytechnic today. Are you studying for the exams?'

'Yes, I am.'

'Okay. Run along now. You are going to be late for college.'

Kala nodded and skipped towards the kitchen humming a familiar tune. Natesan smiled as he watched his daughter disappear, and started working on his accounts.

~

The goddess of the day was called Muthumariamman and her abode was near a reservoir in the village of Sirungudi, a few kilometres away. A tempo traveller was arranged for devotees from Ayyanarpatti, and Natesan and Raji took it along with a number of other villagers. Once they reached the temple, Natesan stepped out of the vehicle and looked for his wife. She was the last one to get out of the van as she had the far corner seat. She always took the far corner seat because she didn't like talking to the other women much. It didn't surprise him that she was always the last in the village to know of any gossip.

'Raji, do you have everything you need for the offering?'

'I think so.' She took her rice and flower basket and held it up to him.

'Here, keep some money with you in case you need anything.'

'No, no, I have what I need. Oh…I see the miller and his wife. Let me go before she sees me.'

But it was too late as the old miller had already seen them. He stopped his motorbike next to them and cut the engine. He was about sixty and had an impressive moustache and was hence called Meesa Miller though the primary purpose of the object in question was to frighten his grandchildren, of which there were many. His wife, dressed in a bright parrot-green silk sari and adorned with all the gold that her wide neck could take, gingerly stepped off the bike.

'Your husband didn't bring you on his bike?' she asked Raji, who looked very uncomfortable.

'No, we came in the van,' Raji replied. She slipped off her sandals and walked inside the temple complex swiftly. The miller's wife followed her inside, chattering.

'How are you, thambi?' The miller wasn't going to let him get away easily, Natesan realized. A crowd was beginning to materialize around them. The richest farmer in the ten-kilometre radius and the man most likely to step into that spot. This was going to be fun, the crowd reckoned.

'With your blessings, all is well.'

'Why do you need my blessings? I am an ordinary mortal, so ordinary that I can't even find people to cut my cane and sow the paddy. They get a hundred rupees for free from the government every day that they don't want to work. Have you loaded yours?'

'Natesan transported his last load yesterday.' Natesan turned sharply. Chandran, the village busybody, just the person he didn't need.

'How is it that you cut and shipped your cane while the rest of us are still waiting for farmhands?'

Natesan smiled politely and wondered how he should

reply. What did the miller want him to say? Because I went to the northern villages by myself and spent days bribing and begging farmhands to cut my cane. Because I bribed the lorry driver to take my load to Madurai. None of you were willing to come with me to speak to the labourers or pitch in to split the money for the truck. None of you wanted to share the tractor to plough before the sowing. What did they want him to tell them? That he has a magic wand that produces labourers on demand?

Fortunately, the sound of another motorbike provided the much-needed distraction.

'Ah, Councillor Muthu is here. Is that a new bike I see?' Natesan changed the topic.

'Yes, he bought a Thunderbird. He's a real politician now, he can afford it,' the miller informed him drily.

The new arrival parked his bike and looked around. He had put on a few kilos since Natesan had seen him last. A few extra layers of self-importance were evident as well. He was wearing a kara vetti, a dhoti with a three-coloured border signifying the party flag. He pulled up the dhoti as soon as he got off his bike so that if anyone was in doubt over his political affiliations, they wouldn't be any more. He made straight for Meesa Miller and Natesan. Natesan looked for a ring – it was there all right. A gold ring on the third finger of his right hand embossed with a picture of the fearless leader of his political outfit.

'Miller ayya. Glad to see you here. You should come to our party office,' Muthu began respectfully.

The miller laughed. 'You want me to waste my money in one of your elections?' he said and walked away abruptly.

The miller didn't deal with small fish; he went straight to Karuppanan.

Muthu was taken aback but he recovered quickly and turned to Natesan. 'Anna, how are you? We haven't met in a long time.'

'Yes, Muthu. I never see you in the village or the co-op.'

'I'm extremely busy with party meetings. The district elections are coming up and the party secretary was here last week. Very busy time for us party workers.'

'Have you heard from Mari?' Natesan enquired after Muthu's brother who happened to be in Singapore and who, for the most part, financed Muthu's politics and his lifestyle.

'He is doing well but there's a problem. His visa will expire soon and he'll be back in a few months.'

'What is the problem in that? It's good news that your brother is coming back from Singapore after so many years, isn't it?' Natesan was genuinely puzzled. Usually it was a matter for celebration when the boys came home.

'But this time he doesn't want to go back. There is no future here. What will he do here? You should advise him to go back,' Muthu explained.

Natesan could not believe his ears. He turned away without saying another word. He was reminded of the last time he saw Mari. It was a few years ago at Changi airport when Natesan was coming back for good. Mari came running to security at the last minute to give him two gold chains and cash to take back to his family back home. One of those chains, this thadimadu is wearing around his neck now, he thought indignantly. That poor man is breaking stones in Singapore so that this rascal can play politics on his new bike. And this rascal has the audacity to tell him to convince Mari to go back to Singapore. Shameless!

But Natesan knew very well how the Singapore story worked for most people. The men spent their money drinking and watching the latest Tamil films every weekend. When someone came back home, they bought utterly useless, expensive things from Musthafa market and sent them to their families. Worse, some sent money to all their relatives back in the village who seemed to think that in Singapore money grows on trees. When he had been one of the boys, he told them to save and send money to the bank or to Neru anna but they laughed at him. 'What will you do with all this money?' 'Are you going to become the next miller?' They all came back, one after another, five years after they had left their village, to find that they now had zero savings and families with expensive tastes and the only way to sustain the lifestyle was to go back for the next five years. Five years of breaking and lifting stones in Singapore and all that is left is a colour TV and a wife with saris and jewellery from the latest Nalli Silks billboard. Idiots!

~

It was evening when the tempo dropped Natesan and Raji back home at Ayyanarpatti. The devil wind of Aadi was in full force as they walked back home from the drop-off point.

'You were quiet during the way back. You didn't say a word.'

'Who is saying that?'

'Don't tease me. What's wrong?'

'Nothing is wrong, Raji. You go back home. I feel like a bath.'

'So bathe at home. I'll pull water from the well for you, why go to the kollai in this wind?'

'No, I'll be back soon.'

'Will someone steal our kollai if you don't visit it for a day?'

Natesan smiled at the thought of someone running away carrying his 12.2 acres on their back, perhaps like Hanuman carrying the mountain with the medicinal plant. 'They might. I'll see you at sundown.'

'Have some tea first.'

Natesan shook his head. 'I ate too much at the temple.'

'All right. If Kala comes back early, I'll send tea with her.'

Natesan cut through Thirumalai's farm to get to his. Acres of cane were billowing in the wind. If they didn't cut it soon, it'd go dry and perhaps decay. They had to get farmhands working on it soon, he thought. He crossed the Northern Palm – from here, the land was his. As always, he stopped for a moment to take in his land. The cane was gone and on the eastern side the paddy field still retained some of the water from the morning. The coconut and palm groves were mostly at the western end. Most of the land had been lying barren when he came back from Singapore. Look at it now! Natesan felt the familiar pleasure course through his veins. He walked on. Natesan was planning to go organic in two acres starting this year. He and Raghu had talked about it in detail at the last co-op meeting. The issue though was how to separate the two acres from the rest of the land. Perhaps his periya anna's land behind the Amman temple could serve as a pilot for organic farming. That land wasn't being used for anything now, and it was far away from the rest of the village lands.

'This channel again! Why is it getting blocked every single day? Kala said she fixed it.'

Natesan ran to the pump shed to get his pickaxe. While he was there, he powered on the motor. It was his one indulgence – water drawn from the bore well for no other reason other than to take a bath. Back with the pickaxe, he set to work on the channel. He blocked the broken channel completely, and then cut a separate channel through the cane lands straight to the trees at the south end. There were only a few coconut and nungu palms, and an old mango tree at the south end, but they needed water too. The mango tree especially was a water guzzler. It was said to be the oldest tree in the village and the fruit was pure heaven. That is, when he got his hands on them, which was never, as the village brats were ingenious thieves.

Finished, he walked back to the pump shed. He put the pickaxe back, removed his clothes and climbed into the water tank. The water felt good against his body. He thought of the time when there was no water tank but the well was full of water. Nobody in the village needed a bore well. He and his brothers would dive straight into the well right after eating stolen nungu fruit from their father's trees. It was aeons since they had come here together. For periappa's funeral, yes, that's when they came to the kollai last. Periappa was cremated in his beloved kollai. He wondered whether his brothers ever thought about the kollai. When they visited the village, none of them, even Neru anna, ever bothered to visit the land. Officers and bank managers don't have time to visit the kollai unless it is an old man's funeral or to showcase the rustic rural life to their city friends. Our kollai is just paradise, they say to their friends. Then why don't you move here, Natesan always felt like asking but he never did. His brothers could afford to live in the city and romanticize their rural homeland because they had two extra letters behind their names that Natesan did not have – the degrees they had earned.

Telling him not to give his money for daily interest! How did they think he had recreated this rural paradise that they could now show off to their friends? How else could he have procured the most modern of bore wells in the entire district? None of his brothers had to beat metal. They all had government jobs at twenty-three. At twenty-three, he was in Coimbatore outside periyanna's house beating metal. Periyanna had spoken to his then landlord and found Natesan an empty shed not far from the house. Natesan had made that his metal workshop in the six months he lived there. Every morning, he would walk to the metal stores to find steel. He would spend the rest of the day beating them, moulding them into stainless steel dabbas of various sizes, and in the evening he would go find the welders to put them together. His sister-in-law's friends loved his shiny boxes – how many dabbas he had sold there! When he was there last year for Anand's wedding, twenty years later, they remembered his dabbas. They still use them; they are the best steel dabbas they ever bought. Dabba Natesan, they called him. He looked down at his hands. He had lost a finger at the welding shop in Singapore in his second year there. They sent him to construction after that. No more metal for him.

He wrapped the towel around his waist and stepped out of the tank. He pulled on his underwear from below the towel and tied his dhoti. He removed the towel and looked up at the clothesline the temporary farmhands had put up last week. He walked towards it squeezing water out of the towel. He spread the towel, shook it twice, and reached up towards the clothes line. The wind caught the towel and carried it several inches higher that he had intended. The last thing Natesan heard before the wet towel hit the leaking 11KV electric wire meant to keep out monkeys and peacocks was the jingle of the bicycle bell.

Kala found her father moments later. She dropped the stainless steel teapot and screamed. She ran towards her father but she had the sense not to touch him. Back home in their house, Raji looked on in shock as the grindstone moved in the Aadi wind.

Prelude to a Wedding

The Avani Ayyanar festival was a few hours away but there was no sign of festivities or festival-goers on the road leading to the village temple. Speakers were installed on poles on the sides of the road at regular intervals but they were eerily quiet. Like everyone else, they seemed to be saving their energy for the all-night festivities though the reality was that there was not enough power to go around in these days of eighteen-hour power cuts and the generator hadn't arrived from town yet. The stretch was as deserted as ever when Nithya turned the corner from the state highway on to the road in her TVS XL Super at twice the recommended speed. There was a series of screeching sounds and the decrepit vehicle slowed down of its own accord. Nithya raised the accelerator but the much overworked engine spluttered and in a few moments came to a complete stop. Priya hopped down from the pillion seat on to the road. Nithya kicked the starter hard but it was of no use. The vehicle had given up.

'I can't believe the darn thing just stopped!'

'Are you going to get into trouble for this?'

Nithya had 'borrowed' the moped for the day from her

father, who was conveniently out of town. No one except her mother knew that the girls had taken it to college.

'I don't get into trouble – it's not in my dictionary.' Nithya waved her hand dismissively. 'Thank Pillayar that we are nearly home. Let's roll it back.'

She started pulling the vehicle along on her side while Priya grabbed the carrier handle and pushed it from behind. It was slow going but the girls didn't complain. They had shown off the XL Super to their friends in college. Nithya had even secured an honorary position among the biker boys for expertly driving a motorcycle that was clearly well past its expiry date.

'We'll be late for the temple,' Priya said, worriedly, as they crossed the long line of eucalyptus trees. Nithya had given the festival adequate publicity in college by starting a rumour that the Ayyanar of Ayyanarpatti, he who stood outside the Durga temple, specialized in bringing true lovers together, and as a result the girls were expecting a busload of their college mates to turn up.

'Don't worry, they won't reach the village until eight or so and it's not even six. In any case, Ashok will wait.' Ashok was a senior in college who, Nithya was certain, had a crush on Priya.

'I don't ca—' She was interrupted by the ring of her cellphone. Nithya slowed down to let her friend answer but Priya pretended not to hear it.

'You've been ignoring your Ravi machan the whole day.'

Priya glared at her. 'I don't know why he keeps calling.'

'Who else will he talk to if not the girl he's going to marry?'

'We aren't getting married…'

'He's not going to wait forever. He has already waited so many years. He must be what, thirty now?'

Priya turned pale, and Nithya bit her tongue and moved in quickly to limit the damage.

'I didn't mean it that way,' she said earnestly. 'So what if he's thirty? He's wealthy and he really likes you. There are lots of girls who get married to really old men. Do you remember the film where…' Nithya stopped in mid-sentence as the realization dawned on her that she was digging an even deeper hole.

Priya had stopped pushing the motorcycle. 'I am not getting married. How many more times do I need to tell you before you'll believe me?' Priya started walking away.

Nithya stared at her friend's back in astonishment. So bloody sensitive these girls were! She couldn't believe that Priya was leaving her to roll the motorcycle all by herself. Now it was going to take her forever to get home, though, on second thoughts, she concluded that it may not be such a bad thing. She had suddenly developed a prescient feeling that her father may have come back home early. She had forgotten that he made it a point to be in the village for the festival. She parked the vehicle under the banyan tree on the roadside and sat down on a boulder to ponder over her next move. She would need nothing short of a miracle to extricate herself from the situation if the paterfamilias was indeed home.

She pulled out her phone to place a discreet call to her mother's cellphone when she heard a car behind her, turning on to the village road. She cursed aloud. That was, in all probability, her father being dropped off by his colleagues. But before she could turn around to confirm her suspicions, she noticed Priya running back towards her. As she looked on, Priya ran behind the banyan tree and stayed there, hidden from view. The car was close now, and Nithya turned around. Why was Priya hiding from her father? She didn't borrow the TVS, did she?

The Honda City slowed down and Nithya recognized the driver. Of course! She was now in the unenviable position of being caught in a lovers' tiff.

'Hello!' Ravi called out to her as he rolled down the window. 'Where is your friend?'

'She is ill. When did you come from Chennai?'

'This morning. I came to talk to her. Will you tell her to stop avoiding me?'

'Sure…I mean, she isn't avoiding you. Why would she?'

'You tell me.' He pointed at the TVS XL Super. 'Does that piece of scrap work?'

Nithya looked at him hatefully. 'It is not a piece of scrap. I take it to college every day.'

'Really?' Ravi looked at the object of discussion curiously for a few moments. 'What are you doing here?'

'I like resting under this banyan tree on my way back home. It helps me collect my thoughts,' Nithya explained as if it was the most natural thing in the world.

Ravi's eyes narrowed, and he stared hard at the tree for a few moments while Priya held her breath and Nithya looked totally unconcerned. 'Ask your friend to call me,' he said finally and pulled away.

Nithya watched the car go past the turn into the village,

heading straight for the mango grove. She got up and, without a second glance at the banyan tree, started pulling the XL Super along with her. A minute later, she felt someone pushing it from behind.

'Thank you,' Priya said.

Nithya did not reply. She wanted to find out what was going on between the two but she didn't fancy herself as the swan that carried messages from Nala to Damayanti and back. She would rather be the ugly duckling who pushed the heavy motorcycle home by itself. They continued silently until the final bend into Ayyanarpatti where Priya turned off towards her house leaving Nithya to face the music.

It is tempting to stay with the duckling and find out how she fared but this is not her story. She is the lucky one.

~

As the girls were making their way through the village road, Vijaya kept looking at the wall clock every two minutes, wondering why her daughter hadn't reached home yet. She had tried calling but the call wasn't going through. She was about to step out of the house and go towards the main road when the phone rang. Hardly anyone called the landline these days and she was certain it would be a telemarketer.

'Hello?'

'Hello, athai, is Priya at home?'

Vijaya now wished it was the telesalesman. At least she could give him a piece of her mind. She took a moment to steady her voice.

'No, she isn't back from college.'

'But it's late and she's not picking up her phone,' Ravi said, concerned. 'Aren't you worried?'

'No,' she replied.

'You don't know how unsafe it is for girls nowadays.'

'She's fine. There are other girls in the village with her.'

'Well, she isn't with Nithya. I don't think that you people understand...'

Vijaya ended the call and put the receiver back in the cradle. She hesitated, lifted the receiver and put it back down at an angle such that it didn't quite fit. Ravi wouldn't be calling back for a while, not on this phone. She proceeded to switch on the TV. The mega serials were just beginning but her mind wasn't on them. In fact, she had a reputation in the village for always watching TV but still being unable to provide updates on any of the serials. The TV was her way of ensuring that no one spoke to her unnecessarily. Her thoughts turned to Ravi's call. She cursed her fate for having to be polite to the bastard, to watch in the sidelines as her daughter was made the sacrificial lamb in the family's own soap opera.

Her daughter! Priya wasn't home yet! She rushed to the door for the second time when her cellphone rang. Her husband.

'Hello.'

'Are you the district collector?'

'Huh?'

'What's keeping you so busy?'

'You take care of the housework and perhaps you'll know,' she snapped back.

'Don't you talk back at me. How dare you cut the line when Ravi called?'

'It got disconnected,' Vijaya lied. It didn't take long for that little twit to complain to his uncle.

'Don't make excuses. He called to check on Priya as she wasn't answering her phone. He has her best interests in mind,' her husband reminded her.

'He has more than her best interests in his mind and you know it too.'

'Vijaya!'

She did not reply and he continued, 'He is going to be our son-in-law soon. When he speaks to you, you speak. Do you understand me?'

'No, I don't.' She pressed the end button on the phone. She was too angry to be intimidated by her husband. She had also reached the conclusion that she didn't have much to lose in this game. She knew what was in store for her later that night – a few taunts, a couple of slaps, name-calling of her family – but it didn't matter any more. Her husband had stopped mattering to her years ago. How could she care about a man who didn't hesitate to pimp out his daughter?

It had started innocuously enough soon after Priya was born. The old matriarch of the house, Priya's great-grandmother, used to put the baby to bed telling her stories of how her machan, her aunt's son, would come in a horse to marry her when she grew up. She had laughed it off as the machan in question was a boy of twelve and the bride was a few weeks old. But before long, everyone else in the family started referring to Ravi as Priya's future husband. Vijaya knew that the family had been incestuous for generations and she was one of the rare outsiders. When Ravi came to the village for his school holidays, the boy was teased endlessly and asked to take care of his bride. By the time Priya turned five, Vijaya was convinced that the environment wasn't healthy for her daughter and made an attempt to send her to a residential school. She was overruled.

Things seemed to get better once the old woman passed away, and for a while everyone was busy with their own lives. Vijaya became less paranoid about her family's intentions but things started going downhill once Priya hit puberty. The family and by extension the villagers treated her as a bride-in-waiting. Ravi, who had largely ignored her for several years, started calling her every day and there was nothing Vijaya could do about it as everyone else thought it was as it should be. For the past few years, Vijaya had fought tooth and nail to secure an education for her daughter against intense pressure to stop her studies and get her married to Ravi who was fast approaching thirty.

'Amma!' Priya entered the house, looking exhausted. 'You won't believe what Nithya…'

'Ravi said you were not with Nithya.'

'How does he know where I am? And why does he keep following me? I don't want to talk to him!'

Vijaya beamed. Priya didn't want to speak to Ravi. That suited her perfectly fine. That's how things should have been in the first place. Mother and daughter spent the next hour trying on saris and jewellery to wear to the night's festival, and Priya finally decided on a deep-red silk sari and her great-grandmother's ruby necklace. She hadn't yet mastered the art of tying a sari and her mother helped her, aided by tens of safety pins, while Priya entertained her with the story of Nithya and her broken-down moped.

Vijaya laughed a lot that evening; she had been planning on using the menstrual excuse to get out of visiting the temple but her daughter had put her in good spirits. She would go to the festival, light lamps and pray for everyone's health. Perhaps her daughter would have a real future, she hoped, as she chose a dazzling yellow silk sari with a broad golden border for herself, very unlike the neutral saris that she was usually seen in.

Vijaya and Priya left for the temple, holding hands, giggling like school girls.

~

'Machan, when is the wedding?' Vivek, the new arrival, asked Ravi.

The men were sitting around a small table in the dilapidated shed at one end of the mango grove. Not long ago, the shed had hosted the switchboard and controls for the motor pump but the bore well had dried up, making the shed redundant. Nowadays, that was where the young men hung out to drink during weddings and festivals, away from the prying eyes of the women, not to mention the older crowd who drank closer to home but frowned upon anyone else who dared to do the same.

Ravi took a large mouthful of the Chivas that one of the Singapore returnees had brought back, and slammed the empty glass down on the table.

'Don't ask him. Can't you see he's already in pain?'

Ravi looked around the table. These were boys he had grown up with, boys who were now men with jobs, businesses, families. Ravi had spent his holidays as a young lad in the village with this group. He was the boy who the others had looked up to, the boy from the city who brought with him stories of exotic streets and hotels, films and celebrities and, most important of all, uninhibited girls. The adulation had died down as they grew up, and as the village bumpkins discovered the world beyond, but Ravi was still respected as the successful city-bred young man who didn't forget his roots. Until now. Now, he was the laughing stock of Ayyanarpatti.

The wedding cards were printed, the venue booked for both wedding and the reception, and then his bride didn't want to get married. He couldn't believe his ears when his parents told him. He had waited patiently for her all his life and Priya had dashed his dreams. He was convinced she was very much in love with him but her mother, his aunt who had always hated him, must have turned her against him. College was a mistake, he knew now. He should have listened to his parents and married her before she started college. That way, she wouldn't be insisting on finishing her studies before thinking of marriage. What was there to think about anyway? He had promised her the world – a new flat so that she wouldn't have to stay with his parents, a car and a chauffeur at her disposal, and he had even agreed to let her continue her education. But it was futile. She was adamant, and her grandfather had given in to her wishes. Since then, she had been avoiding him and not answering his calls.

'How could you give her up, machan?'

'I haven't given her up.'

He got up abruptly and left the shed. He needed fresh air. Nobody stopped him.

Why this kolaveri, kolaveri di?

Ravi laughed bitterly as he heard the loudspeakers from the temple yard blaring out the song. He wondered if Ayyanar, in whose honour the festival was being celebrated, was going through the same murderous rage towards his consort. He started walking towards the direction of the temple. He had to find Priya and speak to her. He had to make her understand.

~

'Don't look behind but he is there!' Nithya whispered. The two girls were standing near the temple tank, watching the procession of married women carrying lamps to be lit in the water. Priya wasn't sure if Nithya meant Ashok or Ravi, and so she ignored the comment.

'Things okay at home?'

'Serious trouble. TVS and bicycle ban for the rest of the year, only bus.' Nithya said, looking glum. That wasn't all. Her father had promised that he would also inform Priya's parents but she decided that there was no point in alarming her friend.

'Oh hello,' Ashok called out from behind them. The girls turned around, pretending to be surprised.

'This is your village?' The question was addressed to both of them though he had eyes only for Priya.

'Do you always ask questions for which you already know the answers?' Nithya asked him. Ashok flushed and Priya giggled.

A boy of about ten came running towards Nithya. 'Amma's calling for you to offer prayers in the sanctum.' He tugged at her sari.

'It's going to come off, you idiot!' she scolded the boy and turned to Priya. 'I'll say hello to Mr Ayyanar and be right back.' Nithya deftly pulled up her sari with one hand, and bolted along with the boy. Priya and Ashok stood in silence for a few seconds.

'Yes, this is my village,' Priya said finally.

'Like she said, I knew that already.'

'I know.'

'You…you look pretty in a sari,' he stammered.

'Thanks.'

'Priya!'

Ravi!

Priya whirled around, stunned, guilt written all over her face. She had been avoiding him all day certain he would try to talk her into marriage and she knew he could be very persuasive.

'Who is this?' Ravi demanded, looking at Ashok suspiciously.

'He is from my college,' she said. 'Ashok.'

'Hello,' Ashok said. 'I ought to be going. Good to see you.' He melted into the crowd.

'Come, let's have a proper talk.' He touched her arm; she quickly pulled away. But she followed him when he walked towards the tamarind grove that abutted the temple premises. They left the crowds behind and were soon out of earshot. Ravi sat down on a boulder under one of the trees. Priya remained standing, leaning against a low branch.

'So, who is he?' Ravi asked, his voice slurring.

'I told you, he's from my college.'

'Which year?'

'Third.'

'How do you know him if he's not in your year?'

'He…I don't remember how he…we met.'

'I see. Why was he talking to you?'

'He came to say hello. But why are you asking all these questions? He is a boy from college, that's all.'

Ravi got up and walked towards her. 'I'm beginning to see why you didn't want to get married. You wouldn't be able to frolic with senior boys, would you?'

'He was just…'

'Don't lie to me,' he hissed. She could smell the alcohol in his breath. She took a step back. He grabbed her arms.

'Let me go. You are hurting me.'

Ravi tightened his grip. 'You are not going anywhere. I am not going to wait for you, not any more. Do you understand me?'

Priya looked at him, puzzlement turning to shock and disbelief as comprehension hit her. This was not the man who loved her. It must be the alcohol. She tried to free herself but he was too strong for her. He brought her closer and forced his mouth on hers. She bit his tongue and when he pulled out in pain, she screamed. Her screams drowned in the ringing of the temple bells. The festival had begun in earnest.

~

Vijaya was offering thanks in the sanctum when Nithya sought her out. Ayyanar deserved her gratitude for granting her a reprieve, however temporary. Only a couple of weeks ago, she had thought that all was lost when Neru anna called her discreetly to inform her that her family had fixed a wedding date two months out and that arrangements were in full swing. Neru knew her views on the marriage and wanted to give her advance notice.

Vijaya was distraught as she had not anticipated that this would happen so soon. Marrying off her teenage daughter to a thirty-year-old cousin with no real education, and consigning her to a lifetime of blowing the kitchen stove wasn't what she had in mind for her only child. She had beseeched Neru to delay the event and give her some time but he was helpless. He was only the messenger.

When the family broached the subject with Priya two days ago, to everyone's surprise the soft-spoken girl had put her foot down, quietly but firmly. She spoke to her grandfather and explained that she would not get married until she finished her studies. She wasn't going to be the girl who dropped out of college because her in-laws did not want her to study. Or the girl who came to college after her wedding but never had any fun. Her grandfather knew there was no point in trying to reason with a seventeen-year-old and reluctantly agreed to Priya's wishes. The wedding was postponed indefinitely though Vijaya knew it was only a matter of time before they brought it up again. But on the bright side, her daughter didn't even want to speak to Ravi! That was reason enough to thank all the gods in the world.

'Is Priya with you, aunty? I can't find her.'

Vijaya looked up at Nithya in surprise. She had naturally assumed her daughter was with her friends. Priya wasn't the sort who would go away by herself. Even if she did, the village was safe. They both attempted calling Priya's mobile but there was no answer. Vijaya hurried home while Nithya looked for her in the festival complex.

Vijaya found her daughter crouched in her room, dishevelled, violated, cowering in fright. She had been raped and casually dropped home by her future husband. Vijaya went looking for Ravi, a kitchen knife in hand, but he had already retired to the mango grove to boast of his exploits. Vijaya's husband found her brandishing her knife like a madwoman, running down Upper Street. He took a few nicks before he got her under control.

The wedding was fixed for an auspicious day a few weeks away. Nithya, banned from visiting Priya, took no notice and climbed more than a few walls to talk to her friend but Priya wouldn't say a word, and she finally gave up. Vijaya was locked up in a room by herself for days before the wedding. Priya came to see Vijaya the night before her wedding. She told her mother that she wanted the marriage, and that the wedding was taking place as per her wishes. Vijaya wept but she wasn't sure for whom. She attended the wedding the next day, taking her place in the rituals dutifully. Priya left for Chennai the day after.

A couple of months later, on a visit back home, Priya reassured her mother that she was happy in her marital home. Ravi had apologized a million times for his behaviour, and was always gentle and kind with her. She told her that she was pregnant and hadn't yet informed anyone else. Mother and daughter agreed to abort the fetus if it happened to be a girl. They couldn't find one good reason to raise a girl in their family.

A Love Story, Starring Councillor Muthu

An unsuspecting visitor travelling by road between Rayavaram and Karaikudi is sure to encounter, dotted among the vast stretch of barren land that was once dense forests or arable fields, a number of enclosed properties bound by rather conspicuous walls painted in hues of amber and purple. If the visitor happened to be inquisitive enough to peer into one of these compounds, she will see a number of 60 x 40 square-foot plots laid out in geometric precision.

Layouts.

That ubiquitous Indian phenomenon has not given our little part of the country a miss. Layouts are land parcels that enterprising real estate barons have, over time, bought from nearby villagers at throwaway prices to 'develop' them so that they could then be sold, very often, to the same people at many times the cost. As everyone in the country knows, in our times, the real money happened to be in real estate.

One hot Purataci afternoon, in one such layout between Ayyanarpatti and Rayavaram town, a handful of men wielding pickaxes were busy at work. Our curious visitor, if she were to stop at this particular site, would have been surprised to see that they seemed to be pulling out plot markers and boundary stones from the ground and strewing them all over the layout in a haphazard fashion. There was also a lookout standing apart from the group, next to the main road.

'Chandran anna,' one of the boys asked the lookout, 'why are we pulling out these boundary stones?'

'That rascal Bai cheated our Karuppanan,' Chandran replied. 'Bai bought this land from him and developed it but he did not pay Karuppanan the agreed price.' Karuppanan was the district secretary of the ruling political party, the same outfit that the motley group of men on the site were affiliated with.

'Why did Karuppanan sign the sale agreement if he didn't get the money?' asked the boy, puzzled.

'You don't need to know all the history. Go back to work,' Chandran snapped. The boy made a face and bent down to pull out another boundary marker.

'But what will this solve? This land is still in Bai's name, isn't it?' someone else asked. The rest of the men stopped working and looked at Chandran expectantly. Their curiosity was piqued as they, not unlike the rest of us, were naturally interested in finding out why they were doing what they were doing.

'This is just a symbolic gesture, a warning – today, we destroy his layout and, tomorrow, we destroy him,' Chandran explained.

'But what if Bai finds out that we are vandalizing his land?'

'Oh, he will find out all right, but he won't dare come here. He's too scared of Karuppanan.'

'Why are you looking out on the road so intently if you are certain Bai's henchmen won't turn up?' That impudent boy again.

'You silly oaf. All of you back to work. No more questions.' Chandran moved away from them and towards the road. The men were looking for a reason not to work and he wasn't going to fall for it, he decided. Wait, did he see someone in the distance? He furrowed his brows and stared. There was definitely a speck heading in his direction. As he watched, the speck slowly became a khaki cycle, or rather, a khaki figure on a bicycle. The postman? It was too late for him. The lineman? It didn't look like the electrician. As the figure came closer, Chandran recognized the khaki uniform. Policeman! Chandran pulled out his phone and dialled urgently.

'Muthu! There is a guy on a bicycle, he looks like a policeman and he is coming towards the layout. What do we do now?'

'Police! Impossible! Karuppanan has already spoken to the police and they aren't supposed to be there. They'll turn their eyes away, this has nothing to do with them,' Muthu said impatiently. Chandran had a reputation for inventing problems where there were none.

'But he looks real, Muthu.'

'Which policeman travels on a bicycle these days? In fact, I am certain that this is one of Bai's men in disguise. Bai must have sent him to find out what we are up to. You know what? You take a couple of men and hold him right there, I'll be there in five minutes,' said Muthu.

'All right, but aren't you in Trichy? How will you get here so soon?'

'No…er…I'm on my way back. Don't worry, I'll be there in no time.'

Muthu was spending the day peacefully and secretively at a friend's house in town. He had harboured no plans of venturing out to the layout, as there was a real risk that Bai would send his men. Councillor Muthu abhorred violence in all forms, especially when it was likely to be directed against him. But from what Chandran was saying, Bai had sent just one guy. It was worth heading to the layout to have a friendly chat with this specimen. That would show the Bai who the kingpin was in this district. Karuppanan would be pleased as well. He took his leave and set out on his motorbike.

Meanwhile, the man dressed as a cop, and who was in fact a real cop, Constable Sambu, slowly rode his bicycle, whistling tunelessly, and looking curiously at the men at work in the layout. He was returning from his usual mid-afternoon tryst with his young mistress who lived nearby, and he took the roundabout route to avoid passing by his home on his way back to the town police station. He had never seen so many men in the layout since Bai bought the land nearly a year ago now. He was wondering whether he should stop by and find out what they were doing there when he noticed a man on the roadside waving at him. He looked closely to see if it was someone he knew. It wasn't. A few of the other men from the site had also come out to the road and they were blocking his way! He looked down to make sure he was wearing his uniform. He was. He was taken aback. These men were forcibly stopping a policeman. What audacity!

'Hey, you. What do you think you are doing? Can't you see who I am? I am a policeman.'

'You, a policeman? I must be the chief minister then!' Everyone laughed except Sambu, who was not amused, to say the least.

He stopped his bicycle and dismounted. 'Who are you guys? I'll lock all of you up and break your knees.' Sambu spoke in his most authoritative voice, but it was of no use.

'We all know which side of the lock-up you spend time in. Tell us, where did you rent this costume from?' Chandran pulled at his lapels. Sambu moved away, astonished. Nobody had ever treated him like this. Not when he was in uniform, at any rate.

'Is that a real moustache? Let me see.' One of the men reached out to pull his moustache. Sambu stepped back and cursed himself for not having his rifle with him. He reached into his pocket to pull out his mobile but Chandran was too quick for him and grabbed his hand. Sambu, now seriously concerned for his personal safety, was pondering over his next move when he heard a motorbike in the distance.

'Muthu is here!' Chandran exclaimed.

Sambu heaved a sigh of relief. Councillor Muthu and he knew each other. But wait, were these Muthu's men? Why were they attacking him? What was Muthu up to?

Muthu stopped his bike and walked over to where the men were standing. As he came closer, the menacing expression on his face turned first to disbelief and then to horror as he realized the magnitude of his mistake. He swallowed.

'I am sorry, constable sir,' he began.

~

The next day, a sweaty Muthu fanned himself with the *Daily Thanthi* as he waited in the veranda of Karuppanan's mansion, waiting for the district secretary to arrive. The leader's wife informed Muthu that her husband had gone to meet the former state secretary, who happened to hail from the same district. Muthu detected an unfamiliar coldness in her usually warm voice. In addition, he hadn't been offered tea or invited inside the air-conditioned house, which was rather worrying.

The Audi Q5 sounded the horn, and the watchman rushed to open the gate and let the car inside. Vinod, another of the leader's sidekicks, opened the front passenger door before the car came to a complete stop, and stood poised to open the back door. Muthu and Vinod looked at each other in mutual distaste. The leader's right and left hands didn't get along with each other for obvious reasons.

Karuppanan alighted from the back seat. He was tall and gaunt, his attire was all khadi, and his forehead was smeared with holy ash from the morning visit to the Sivan temple.

'You imbecile!' Karuppanan roared at Muthu as soon as he noticed him. Muthu dropped the newspaper and took a step back in alarm. This was more serious than he had anticipated.

'Of all the people you could get into trouble with, you threatened a policeman?'

'It wasn't me, anna, and the men didn't know he was a

policeman,' Muthu started his well-practised explanation.

'Don't give me ridiculous excuses. They were your men. And I heard the policeman wasn't even in mufti!'

Vinod stood behind the leader, biting his nails, a nasty smirk on his pockmarked face. Karuppanan continued, 'Do you know where I'm coming from? That town inspector, Kalavati, she came to the state secretary's house, and I had to apologize to her. Did you hear me? I had to say sorry to that bitch.'

'But anna, Muthu didn't know. Please do forgive him,' Vinod pretended to jump to his rescue. Muthu looked at his rival in unconcealed anger.

'Why are you looking at him? I should have given him the job yesterday, and he wouldn't have botched it up like you did. Now that bastard Bai is laughing at me, and that inspector is gloating. My honour is swinging in the wind!'

'It won't happen again. I will get the men and fix this immediately...'

Karuppanan shook his head vehemently. 'No, you are going to do nothing. Vinod will finish the job. You go home.'

'But anna, just let me...' Muthu pleaded.

'Don't show your face to me. Go hide in that village of yours until I call for you. Do you understand me?'

Muthu knew it was futile to argue his case at the current moment especially when he didn't have a case. He touched the leader's feet and crept away without a word. He would have to wait for a more opportune time to beg the leader's forgiveness.

~

Back home in Ayyanarpatti, Muthu sat on the veranda and hid his face behind the newspaper that he'd been reading since the morning. His mother shouted at him for the fifteenth time that day. He knew his family was losing their patience and he couldn't blame them – they had waited patiently on the sidelines for over a decade as he tried to build his political career. He readily admitted that he had made a few wrong choices in the past ten years, but then who hadn't, in politics? Everyone, at some point in their career, had supported one wrong horse or another and learnt the hard way. Only in his case, there were too many wrong horses. He wasn't a good gambler, that was all there was to it. Over the last couple of years, however, things had moved in the right direction for him. A significant reason for this was Karuppanan's patronage. He was now a councillor; construction had started on the Pillayar temple due to his hard work; and more important, he was finally beginning to see some money and earn a bit of respect in the community. Even in Ayyanarpatti, where the villagers had been dismissive of him in the past, they started treating him with respect. Just when things were going so well, this Bai land debacle had happened, and now he had to contend with Karuppanan's displeasure. He knew that wily Vinod was playing a double game to oust him from what he had assumed was his unassailable position as the leader's right-hand man, but there was nothing he could do about it now that he wasn't allowed to see Karuppanan. Depressed, he put the newspaper down and walked to Balu's tea stall. There was no chance of getting another cup of tea at home.

'Anna,' Balu greeted him. There was no one else at the tea stall. 'Please sit down. It's nice to see you here every day.'

Muthu knew that Balu knew that there was a party procession in Trichy that day and the regulars had all gone away to attend. However, appearances had to be kept up.

'Oh, didn't I tell you? I've decided to spend more time in the village, like what Gandhi used to do. India lives in her villages, he used to say. A great man!'

Balu bit back the retort that rose automatically to his tongue. His daily collection had improved due to Muthu's sustained presence in the tea shop over the past week, and he didn't want to rock that boat. Muthu sipped his tea as he watched a handful of young men walk towards the village from the bus stop. It was the college-going crowd heading back home from the umpteen colleges that dot the district. The girls would have come back an hour or so earlier.

'Hey, is that a real policeman or a fake policeman?' one of the young men shouted as they passed the tea stall. The rest of them guffawed. Muthu got up from his seat spilling his tea, and ran after the boys but they had already scampered. Muthu came back to the stall and sat down.

'Ruffians! The youth of today have no respect for anyone,' he muttered. Balu nodded and Muthu continued to rant. 'All they do is mock elders, watch films and go after girls.'

'Sometimes, not even the right girls,' Balu, the omniscient, said sagely. Muthu's ears perked up instantly. He hadn't heard good old village gossip in a while and here was his opportunity to catch up.

'Who may you be referring to?' he enquired casually.

'Subbu, Govindan's son. The word on the street is that he

has caught hold of a fleshy tamarind branch. A very tangy one by all accounts,' Balu said, a hint of mystery in his voice.

'I wouldn't pay much attention to these film-style romances. A girl a day is their philosophy,' Muthu said carefully.

'But this one could turn worryingly serious. Subbu is determined, his friends say.'

'Who is this tangy tamarind fruit?' Muthu was nearly dying of curiosity.

'Someone you may be interested in. Let's say that it's not someone your Karuppanan particularly cares about.'

Karuppanan? What has this got to do with Karuppanan? Muthu had merely intended to while away some time on village gossip, but this was proving to be way more interesting.

'Don't keep me in suspense, Balu. This could be serious, and I may have to get involved to resolve the issue.' Muthu's natural pomposity was back.

'Well, Subbu goes to the college near Thirumayam, where the Bai's daughter also studies.' Balu had stretched out the story long enough.

Muthu's jaw dropped and he stared at Balu in utter disbelief. 'The Bai's daughter? They will cut off his body parts one by one and bury them individually in every pilgrimage town in the country! He doesn't know who he is playing with.'

'As I said, he is very stubborn.'

Muthu's mind went into overdrive as he was acutely aware that this could be the opportunity that he was looking for to get back into Karuppanan's good books. He thanked

Balu profusely for the tea, paid him whatever was left in his pocket and left.

~

A few days later, Muthu found himself once again in the veranda of Karuppanan's house, fanning himself with a newspaper. This time, however, he had done his homework and wasn't the least bit concerned. He had Subbu followed the past several days and received confirmation that the word on the street was indeed true. He had swallowed his pride and befriended a few of Subbu's friends to gather inside information. From all accounts, Subbu and Nafisa were truly, madly, deeply in love. A latter day Romeo–Juliet or, closer to home, Ambikavati–Amaravati, everyone concurred. The couple were waiting for Subbu to finish the semester and start working in Chennai before informing their respective families. Nafisa was rightly worried, and was pushing for an elopement, knowing fully well that her family would not give their consent. More likely, they would simply murder the lovers. Subbu, the optimistic half of the couple and avid film-goer, had not yet lost hope, however. He was waiting for the right moment to talk to the Bai, and convince him of his love for Nafisa, unaware that his life was on borrowed time. The lovers' friends were worried, but they were willing to do everything in their power to unite the lovelorn couple.

Armed with this information, Muthu had waited for the right time to meet Karuppanan, and he found it on one such day when he knew that Vinod had been dispatched to Chennai on an errand.

'Muthu,' the leader looked up, surprised. 'What are you doing here?'

'Anna, I came to tell you a love story,' Muthu said, his eyes gleaming.

'Why, have you gone back to pimping?' Karuppanan demanded. Muthu's face flushed in anger but he controlled himself. Karuppanan was unnecessarily raking up the past. Of course, he had arranged and driven a number of women to party offices and guest houses over the years. It was part of the job description and shouldn't be held against him.

'No, but you have to listen to this love story,' he insisted calmly.

Karuppanan looked at him strangely for a moment. 'Muthu, go home and rest for a few weeks. Don't worry about anything,' he said gently as if speaking to a mentally unstable person.

'All right, if you don't want to listen, I am taking the story to Bai,' Muthu turned around dramatically, pretending to leave. 'He would want to hear this, for sure.'

'Bai!' the leader exclaimed. 'Wait. What has this got to do with him?'

Muthu smiled and came closer to Karuppanan. 'Bai's daughter is the heroine of this particular romance. The boy is from my village,' he whispered.

'But there are no Muslims in your village,' the leader pointed out the obvious.

'Exactly,' Muthu echoed.

Karuppanan laughed and rubbed his hands in glee. 'Muthu, you have brought us a goldmine! Padma,' he shouted for his wife. 'Bring some tea and snacks. Sit down, my boy. We need to talk.'

Life was looking up for Muthu.

Muthu left Karuppanan's mansion a few hours later. The leader's instructions were succinct and clear. Muthu was not to contact him directly in the next few weeks even if it was an emergency. The date for action was set after much discussion. There were special prayers at the mosque the following Friday, which most of the men would attend and, therefore, was perfect timing. Karuppanan's objective was simple. Bai should lose his honour and shouldn't be able to show his face in public any more. Vinod and Muthu were jointly in charge of the execution. Karuppanan would brief Vinod as soon as he arrived from Chennai. Muthu wasn't pleased at the joint charge but he knew this was a test, a trial by fire, and he was determined to come out of it intact.

Muthu's primary task was to out the lovers. He and a group of party workers would turn up unexpectedly at the college coffee shack where Subbu and Nafisa spent time together. Their friends would be called away one by one on some errand or another. When the party workers entered the shack, Subbu and Nafisa would be alone. A photographer would take a few shots, and the couple would be dragged to the local police station by Muthu and his men. Subbu would be arrested and Nafisa let off with a warning; Karuppanan would take care of the police. Thirumayam thankfully didn't fall under Kalavati's authority and Karuppanan had a freer rein. The party workers would then parade Nafisa to her house. This alone would be too much for the Bai, but more was yet to come.

Vinod and his men would be ready, waiting for the call from Muthu. Just as the procession left the station for Bai's home, Vinod and his men would start burning Muslim homes in Karim Nagar. It was close enough to Bai's house but his house would not be touched. Bai was the wrong class. A dozen or so Hindu houses in the neighbourhood would also be targeted so that it looked like an even assault. Every detail was planned.

On his way back home, Muthu dropped by Balu's tea stall and ordered tea. As usual, Subbu and his friends passed by but they didn't taunt him. Some of them were his friends now and they waved, but Muthu did not acknowledge them. He was feeling uneasy about the direct action planned for the following Friday. The plan had sounded perfect when he was talking to Karuppanan. It was just the thing he needed. But back in the village, watching young Subbu walk home without an inkling of the catastrophe that was going to befall him, Muthu wasn't so sure any more. It was one thing to pull out stones from Bai's land, but it was something else altogether to drive the young lovers to suicide, and burn a number of impoverished homes. He wasn't a particularly honest man, there wasn't a single one in the profession he was in, but he wasn't a murderer and didn't want to be one. However, he knew very well this was his only chance to ingratiate himself with the leader. If he lost this game, it was goodbye to politics for him. And since he wasn't good at anything else, his life was finished. It was a sobering thought.

~

A couple of days before action day, Muthu went to visit the college. He wanted to familiarize himself with the neighbourhood so that if things went wrong, he knew how and where to vanish. He parked his bike in front of the soon-to-be famous coffee shack and went inside. He saw Subbu at a table in the far corner; a girl in a hijab was sitting next to him. As soon as he went inside, a few students from the other tables rushed to Subbu's table and seated themselves around it. Muthu smirked at them knowingly and left the scene.

The next morning, he was in his usual perch at Balu's tea stall when he saw the boys walk towards the bus stop. Subbu was not among them. After they disappeared from sight, Subbu slowly appeared from his house at the far end of Upper Street. Instead of proceeding towards the bus stop, he walked towards the tea stall and sat down on the bench opposite Muthu. Balu looked at the new visitor in surprise while Muthu ignored him altogether.

'Muthu anna...' Subbu began.

Muthu pretended not to have heard him but Subbu continued, 'You have to help me.'

Muthu cringed involuntarily. This was exactly what he didn't want to happen. 'Why don't you go to a fake policeman? I am sure he'd be able to help you.'

'I am sorry, anna, please forgive me. You have to help me, there's no one else,' Subbu pleaded.

'What's the problem?' Muthu asked gruffly.

'You know about me and Nafisa...you don't have to pretend. I know you know. But I have reason to believe that her father has also found out. A number of men have been following us recently.'

'Serves you right for going around with a Muslim girl.'

'Love knows no religion.'

'I bet it will recognize a machete when it sees one. Question is, will you?'

'Please understand me, anna.'

Subbu's voice was so plaintive that Muthu felt sorry for the boy. 'What do you want me to do?'

'Help us! Karuppanan is Bai's enemy, so I thought perhaps he would…'

'He would what?'

'He would protect us. I mean, you could protect us but of course with his blessings.' The poor boy had no idea where the danger to his life and love came from. Muthu was beginning to feel terribly guilty about the charade.

'You think we politicians have no other work than to conduct weddings? You think we are marriage brokers?'

'No, anna.'

'Stop seeing this girl immediately.'

'I'd rather die.' Subbu said it with the elegance and naivety of the young, very much in love.

Muthu snorted and looked at him scornfully though his heart was melting inside. He had to be firm, he told himself.

Subbu got up to leave, as he seemed to have realized that Muthu wasn't going to help him. He started walking dejectedly towards the bus stop. As Muthu watched him go, his whole life flashed before him – like a movie flashback.

He quickly weighed the options in his mind and came to a decision.

'Come back and sit down, boy. Balu, give him a tea and vadai.'

Subbu sat down obediently.

'Now, listen carefully. This is what you are going to do.'

The following day, as planned, Muthu and his men reached the coffee shack to catch the lovers red-handed. Their friends had already been called away. When the men reached the far corner table, they saw two hijab-wearing girls staring at them in shock and indignation. Subbu was nowhere to be seen. The men retreated, not knowing what to do. Muthu called Vinod to inform him that the action was off.

Nafisa did not turn up at college the next day. Or the day after. After a week or so, the word around town was that she had been sent to Chennai to a relative's house and would be completing her studies there. Subbu had vanished from Ayyanarpatti the day before the event, and his family had no idea where he had gone. He called them after a couple of days and informed them he had found gainful employment in Chennai and would not be visiting the village in the near future.

Muthu wasn't seen at Karuppanan's for the next several weeks, as per the leader's instructions. One fine morning, Muthu and his entourage turned up at Pavithran's house. Pavithran happened to be the district secretary of the opposition party. A photo of Muthu prostrating at Pavithran's feet appeared in the local edition of the *Daily*

Thanthi the next day. Muthu had officially defected. Whether Pavithran is another wrong horse remains to be seen.

Our hypothetical visitor would still to be able to see the layout on the road between Ayyanarpatti and Rayavaram town. Bai hasn't been able to sell it yet. The land is registered in his daughter Nafisa's name, and her presence and signature are required for the sale.

Macondo Thatha

Years later, when the little one asked him for the story of his village, he told her about the schools and bridges he had built all over the district; about his eccentric brother Bose and his omnipresent INA rifle; about his envious cousins and their constant threat to his position; of how Durga came to him one day to ask him to build her a temple; and of his all-consuming desire to move away from his roots because he wanted to leave a legacy. He told her everything that was true but not the truth.

He wished for the village he founded to grow into a metropolis, though he admitted that the furthest he had gone was to Thanjavur – the mighty capital of the Chola empire of a thousand years ago, but in his time a dusty town on the high road between Madurai and Madras. He had gone there to bring his younger brother back, the one who had run away in the middle of the night to join the Indian National Army and fight for 'freedom'. He wasn't sure freedom from whom, as he had never felt a lack of it in his affairs, but he was informed that what was being sought by the masses was independence from the British who had enslaved us for centuries. Having never come across a Britisher, he did not share the view of the masses but his young brother, too literate for his own good, thought otherwise. A few years went by without any news of this brother, until one day he received news from the Chettiar in town that the missing man had been seen at an inn in Thanjavur. He went there straight away, met his brother and asked him to come back home. Ramiah, who by then only answered to the name of Bose and would never be parted from his INA rifle, refused to speak of his time in the army, but he did comply with the request and returned home, and remained loyal and steadfast by his brother's side till the very end. On the day when Karuppiah finally left the old village for the new one, for Ayyanarpatti, it was Bose's rifle that carried the day and held his uncles and cousins at bay.

'Don't move,' Bose, a man of few words, commanded and they all listened. Karuppiah left with his wife for the new house his workers had built in a clearing between the old village and town. Bose joined them a few days later. 'The Lone House', they called it, and even now when the official name is Ayyanarpatti and the post office recognizes it as such, older locals still refer to the village as the Lone House Village. Soon after the family moved, the workers arrived with their families and built their houses in the far end of the clearing. Nobody asked them to but they knew their place and knew where to build their dwellings. They were all from Karuppiah's workforce, the families that worked in his farms or at his construction sites, and this was their chance to be closer to town and to work.

But why the lone house? Why not move to town?

He anticipated the question. One evening he was crossing the clearing on his way back home from a site in the nearby taluk when he saw her. As usual, he was dressed in his gold-bordered cotton dhoti and silk shirt, both of which remained spotless even after a long day at the construction site. His walking cane tapped gently on the parched ground when he heard the sound of footsteps walking towards him. The walking cane, a gift from one of his Chettiar clients, was the sole object of contention between him and Bose as it was ostensibly from London, the land of the rulers that Bose had attempted to get independence from. Bose always looked at the object with a distasteful suspicion as if it would turn into a weapon at any moment, and he held his rifle close to him in its presence. The woman, Karuppiah said, reminded him of a girl he had met earlier in the village of Sirungudi, a distant relative, but he soon realized that this woman was nothing like the girl. She was taller than Karuppiah himself, he noticed as she drew nearer, and carried a vel in her hands. In fact, she was no mere woman; this was Goddess Durga herself in person! He was frightened at the thought of her coming to take him away.

But you hadn't done anything wrong, had you?

No, but you never knew what caused the goddess's displeasure. He cowered and dropped to the ground and asked her to spare him. She laughed, and said she hadn't come to kill him, but to ask him a favour – to build a village in this very spot, and build her a temple in that village. He closed his eyes and agreed, and she vanished as swiftly as she had come. He walked home, having resolved to build the lone house immediately.

The little one fell asleep at this critical juncture, which was just as well as this was where he would have had to diverge from the truth. He had another reason to leave the old village; his sons had left to pursue their studies, his daughters were settled with families of their own and it was time for a marriage in the family – his own. Women didn't interest him much, but he believed that a successful man close to the prime age of fifty should take a young wife to cement his status. Why, all his clients in town had more than one wife, and the ones in Singapore and Burma even had foreign wives. He had his eye on his wife's destitute cousin in Sirungudi. Her uncle had approached him to ask if he would take on his niece as a housemaid, but he had a better idea. What better way to give the poor girl a proper life than to marry her? He had discreetly spoken to the man and all was arranged, but he had to be careful that his cousins and uncles did not come to know about it until the wedding was over. They would certainly try to stop it as they did not want any more heirs in the extended family to split the inheritance; there were too many sons as it were. More important, they would all be, without exception, jealous of him – none of them were in a position to take another wife. Durga had made her appearance at just the right time, he decided, and the family soon moved to Ayyanarpatti, to the lone house.

As the day of the wedding drew nearer, he felt a pang of guilt at times at the thought of his dutiful wife having to deal with another woman, but he quickly dismissed the errant thought. He surmised she would be happy enough – she was blessed with five children, two of them sons, and she was getting no younger – it would be a great support to her if the young girl were to come into the household to help her with the work. In any case, he was sure she knew; he had made the arrangements with the priest, the cook, the flower vendor and the musicians in her presence. He had made no pretence at hiding what was going on. It was going to be a simple affair – him, his wife, Bose, his daughters and their families, the bride and her immediate family – that was all. It crossed his mind to notify his sons, but he told himself that they needed to focus on their studies. He also had the feeling that they might not take to the situation benignly. All things considered, it was better to write to them after the wedding.

On the day of the wedding, he offered his morning prayers to Durga, and took out the new clothes that had arrived from the town's tailor the day before. He asked his wife to wear the new sari he had bought especially for the occasion. She looked at the garment quietly, and he told her it was for the best. For years, he had been watching her work herself to death, and he had finally realized that she needed help. He had made the appropriate enquiries, of course, and she could rest assured that this girl was capable of handling the house work while making sure that she respected her elders. His wife nodded sagely but did not say a word. Soon, his daughters arrived with their families, and it was time to leave for the makeshift Durga temple where the wedding would take place. Bose had left for Sirungudi a day earlier as he had the all-important task of bringing the bride along with her family back on the bullock cart. He would bring the bride directly to the temple. It would be inauspicious for her to stop at her future home first.

'Chettiar has asked you to come immediately.'

A messenger from town on a bicycle – this was serious. He explained that he wasn't in a position to be in town until later in the afternoon, but the messenger was insistent. The district magistrate was waiting for him in the Chettiar's house. There were questions around the quality of cement used in building the new bridge, and an anonymous letter had been sent to the magistrate claiming that the bridge would not survive the seasonal rains that year. Karuppiah asked his family to proceed to the temple, and rode back to town with the messenger. They were almost there when he realized that instead of his walking cane he held in his hand Bose's INA rifle. Bose had forgotten to take it to Sirungudi.

It took a few hours before the magistrate was convinced that the anonymous letter had no merit whatsoever. Not only did Karuppiah agree to a stress test of the bridge, he took out Bose's rifle at a particularly emotional point in the discussions, and informed the magistrate that he was willing to shoot himself if the bridge collapsed. The magistrate assured him it was unnecessary. The cyclist offered to drop him back, and they headed for the temple – it was still daylight, the wedding could still happen. To his surprise, however, the only people left in the temple were Durga and Ayyanar, looking rather forlorn. He hurried home on foot, his mind busy with plans for rearranging the wedding.

Alas, it was not to be. At the lone house, the wedding feast was in full swing, and the cook's helpers were busy preparing the night's meal. He was greeted at the door by his beaming wife. She had never looked so happy in all the thirty years he had known her.

'You are finally here! Come inside quickly and bless the newly-weds – I was worried you'd be too late. Thank Durga for everything – you should have seen the girl's face when she found that the groom had been called away. The priest said it was an inauspicious omen, and the poor girl immediately jumped out of the cart and ran to the yeri to drown. None of us knew what to do, but Bose, Bose knew! He ran after her and pulled her out just in time. Oh, it was meant to be. He has given her a life now! Come bless them before it's time to send them away for their first night.'

Karuppiah stared blankly at his wife for a few seconds as he processed the new information. He sighed once he understood, and slowly put the rifle down next to the walking cane by the pillar. He knew when he was outwitted, and it was clear he would have to do what befitted his position. He blessed the newly-weds and announced that his workers would build a house for them next door – that would be his wedding gift. His magnanimity was the talk of the villages in the district for the next several weeks, and there was no repeat of the anonymous letter. He never raised the question of marriage again, and the village of Ayyanarpatti continued to grow.

Acknowledgements

Thanks are due to:

The editors of *Wasafiri* and *Eclectica* in which two of the stories in this collection – 'God's Own Country' and 'A Festive Suicide, Attempted' – appeared first, the former in a different version;

Amit Chaudhuri, for his critique and encouragement, without which this manuscript would have likely languished in the ether;

Romesh Gunesekera, for his perspective on where and how high to aim;

R. Sivapriya, my editor at Juggernaut, for her suggestions and nudges, and more important, for seeing the story behind the stories;

Veena Narayan, Siddhartha Banerjee and Abdullah Khan, fellow writers, for reminding me often that I need to do something with this collection;

Rahul Santhanam, Stuthi Vijayaraghavan and Sridala Swami, friends, for the many conversations bordering on the ridiculous;

My rather large extended family, for their affection and

candour, and large-heartedness in sharing their world with me;

My daughters:

Toshi aka Mallika, for her constant reminders that I really ought to be writing;

Misha, for her impeccable sense of timing;

And finally, Susmit Sarkar, for his thoughtful and carefully phrased suggestions, and for the equanimity with which he plays along whenever I use the 'writing' excuse to extricate myself from my rightful share of household and childcare duties.

A Note on the Author

Veena Muthuraman's stories have been published in *Wasafiri* and *Eclectica*. She lives in Edinburgh and is working on her first novel.

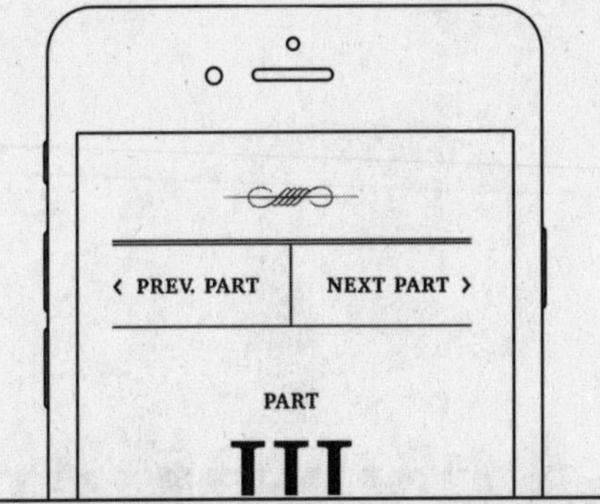

Beautiful Typography

The quality of print transferred to your mobile. Forget ugly PDFs.

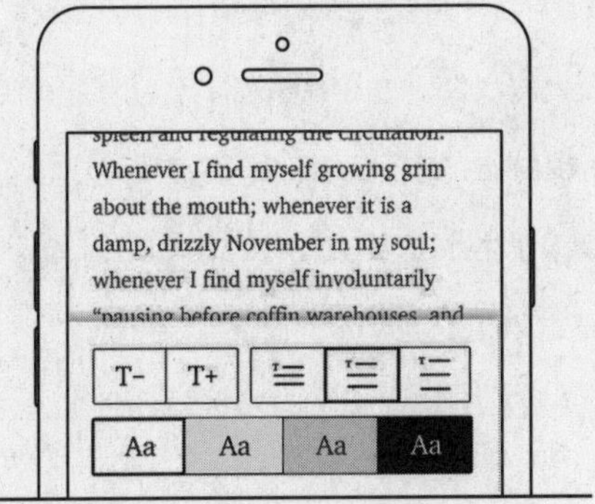

Customizable Reading

Read in the font size, spacing and background of your liking.

AN EXTENSIVE LIBRARY

Including fresh, new, original Juggernaut books from the likes of Sunny Leone, Praveen Swami, Husain Haqqani, Umera Ahmed, Rujuta Diwekar and lots more. Plus, books from partner publishers and loads of free classics. Whichever genre you like, there's a book waiting for you.

CRUCIBLES OF SIN
HITESHA
Can a Geek ever find Love?
Finding Juliet
Toffee
Mary Shelley
Frankenstein
A FAROOQ BUKHARI INVESTIGATION
COLD FLAKE
PRAVEEN SWAMI
A Psychiatrist's Guide To Heartbreak
How to Heal Your Broken Heart
DR SHYAM BHAT
MOIN and THE MONSTER
ANUSHKA RAVISHANKAR
Mafia Queens of Mumbai
stories of women from the ganglands
S. Hussain Zaidi
with Jane Borges
Foreword by Vishal Bharadwaj
Pakistan's Queen of Romance
UMERA AHMED
Nowhere Girl
A Story of Love & Forgiveness
THE BEHEADING
This Is How He Will Bless Her
ABHEEK BARUA
THE Peshwa
The Lion and the Stallion
THE INVISIBLE WOMAN
SAURBH KATYAL
ANGRY BIRDS FAN? READ THE BOOKS!
ANGRY BIRDS TOONS
TOONS TALES
ARCHANA SABOO
ADIKOOL
in
#AfricanAdventures
i am not a bimbette
Tarana Khan
She hates me, He loves me not but...
DON'T FALL IN LOVE
Vandana Shankar
KHUSHWANT SINGH
WE INDIANS

Ask authors questions

Get all your answers from the horse's mouth. Juggernaut authors actually reply to every question they can.

Rate and review

Let everyone know of your favourite reads or critique the finer points of a book – you will be heard in a community of like-minded readers.

Gift books to friends

For a book-lover, there's no nicer gift than a book personally picked. You can even do it anonymously if you like.

Enjoy new book formats

Discover serials released in parts over time, picture books including comics, and story-bundles at discounted rates. And coming soon, audiobooks.

Paytm Wallet, Cards & Apple Payments

On Android, just add a Paytm Wallet once and buy any book with one tap. On iOS, pay with one tap with your iTunes-linked debit/credit card.